Diary of a Motor City
HIT MAN

THE CHESTER WHEELER CAMPBELL STORY

CHRISTIAN CIPOLLINI

Cover by Christian Cipollini
Illustrations by Natasha Cipollini

13-digit ISBN 978-0-985244-06-4
10-digit ISBN 0-9852440-6-2

CONTENTS

MEETING THE DEVIL HEAD ON

"When I hear music, I fear no danger. I am invulnerable. I see no foe. I am related to the earliest times, and to the latest."
- Henry David Thoreau

A COLOSSAL NEW sedan is in full ownership of a virtually empty highway, while the soulful voice of Otis Redding flows from the 8-track player. It's a perfect soundtrack to relax a man on a mission, travelling through the quaint suburbs on a brisk February night. Living it up without a care in the world, nothing can stop this northbound ride on Orchard Lake Road. A journey, no doubt, to a lady friend's abode on nearby Commerce Road.

Cleared for code, Keego Harbor patrol car number 005 heads toward The Palace Restaurant for a much needed night shift lunch break, also travelling along the narrow stretch of Orchard Lake Road - *southbound*. It is 3:19 a.m., and a meeting of extraordinary proportions is about to take place. Neither party is privy, only the powers of fate and destiny are aware of this forthcoming encounter.

The drivers of these two vehicles could never have expected the eventual outcome of their accidental introduction- solemnity crashes into solidarity as simple fender-bender morphs into gangland legend.

CHAPTER ONE

FACT AND FOLKLORE

"If you have a lot of what people want and can't get, then you can supply the demand and shovel in the dough."
– Charles "Lucky" Luciano

WHEN WE THINK of organized crime bosses, drug kingpins, mobsters and professional assassins - geographically speaking – places like New York, Philadelphia, Chicago, Miami or Boston may be the first places that come to mind. For good reason indeed, but there are criminal legends hailing from every major (and plenty of minor) metropolitan areas that are occasionally even more profound than the tales we are familiar with, yet overlooked or simply lacking in much information to warrant spectacular coverage.

Detroit. Now here's a city founded on blue-collar pride - auto capital of the world. From this Michigan powerhouse came some of America's most enjoyed pop culture icons, a professional sports dynasty and one of the most recognizable and respected record labels of all time.

Yes, the same place that once held the unfortunate title of

"murder capital' as well. But Motor City doesn't always come to mind first when the subject of organized crime's most infamous people, places and incidents is proposed. It should. Not because the city deserves a bad rap, no, this city is full of true tales of organized crime and law enforcement - 'good versus evil' stories that are, at times, almost too amazing to be true. But… they are true and should be recognized as important cultural, social and economic variables within American history as a whole.

According to some organized crime historians, such as pointed out in a 2011 CBS Detroit online article by James Buccellato and Scott M. Burnstein – Detroit's organized crime element has actually been quite successful throughout the years. Perhaps, as the piece addresses, that staying under the radar of national publicity was the key. Some inevitably have made headlines of course. There was, in particular, the still-unsolved disappearance of Teamsters boss Jimmy Hoffa.

Though names from the region may not be 'household' to the scale of high profile gangsters Al Capone, Lucky Luciano, John Gotti or Frank Lucas, keeping their *business* in clear view – not notoriety - was the priority. By not garnering so much media and law enforcement attention – they could reach the ultimate goal of earning illicit cash all the more sustainably.

From the brutal Jewish bootlegging bandits known as the Purple Gang to the Italian Mafia's quickness in filling a post-prohibition void with other rackets to narcotics trafficking giving rise to the urban gangster… organized crime has been a constant element. It evolves, it adapts, it builds and it crumbles. The cycle begins again.

Every legend has factual accounts, and plenty of folklore to go with it. It should be noted on the subject of narcotics - and the relationship organized crime has had with it- that 'junk' or 'dope' as a viable contraband source goes back pretty far. The idea of mob bosses not wanting any part of the drug trade, well, that's partially true. Some old school goodfellas did indeed see drugs as nothing but bad publicity, whereas other vices bordered on acceptable. However, let's dispel the myths, stereotypes and non-sensical views - in no uncertain terms: Drugs were dealt even in the glamorous heyday of the Jewish, Italian and Irish gangs. The heroin and powder cocaine invasion, for example, was not a scourge created out of thin air, nor were these poisons exclusive to the inner cities and ghettos. Every ethnic organized crime demographic saw the potential and, at least in part, took to making it work for them.

Simply refer to the conduct of two of New York's most famous mobsters. We're talking about Jack "Legs" Diamond and Charles "Lucky" Luciano, circa 1930. Flanked by three other members, Legs and Lucky would travel by ship to Europe in an effort to secure a narcotics pipeline back to the States. A failed attempt, as noted in author Tim Newark's 2011 Luciano expose titled "Boardwalk Gangster: The Real Lucky Luciano," but a serious effort no less. An endeavor made by an Irish gangster with patent folklore status, and a Sicilian born Mafioso who would go on to change the face and structure of organized crime in America forever. Drugs were most certainly *not* out of the question even for such highly regarded hoodlums, therefore to assume such a societal ill was the product of single ethnic group or specific decade is, quite frankly, ridiculous.

Obviously as the times change, so do the trends of racketeering, the dominant groups in charge, and product of choice. It comes down to basic economics. When a particular immigrant, ethnic or cultural group was downtrodden – there would be splinters that grab onto whatever means necessary to survive.

The groups change and the manner of survival changes, but the common denominator is always cold hard cash and what means are available to bring it in.

The drug trade certainly made the news though. Rules (and yes there were some) that once applied within organized crime all but went out the window by the 1970's. A new era had come to be; one where witnesses, prosecutors, and cops were becoming fair game in the highly profitable narcotics business.

Our story begins in a year that proved quite tumultuous for the Motor City in general. The entire history of our main character didn't start there, but by this time a major turning point in both the legitimate world and *under*world had reared a few ugly heads so to speak. Racial tensions, a continuing energy crisis, economic and social instability at a boiling point, and yes… Teamsters boss Jimmy Hoffa was *taken for a ride* and never came back.

In a place where liquor was once the primary contraband of choice for gangsters to make their fortunes – cocaine and heroin had become king. With the huge amounts of cash flowing from illicit trade also came plenty of corruption. And why did this trade become so lucrative? The story is always the same – if the people, or a segment thereof, feel caught in a hopeless situation - they will seek escape. Heroin, especially, became that escape for many of Detroit's citizens. When so many factors come into play, perhaps it becomes easier to understand how our main character and others like him could even exist.

Again, some of the history and lore may seem surreal, but are actual events. This story is one of them. Meet an almost mytho-logical character; shadowy and cold, but oddly similar to any-body else, in terms of everyday routines. For those that knew of him and his sinister reputation – well, it's the stuff of gangland legend. This is the tale of Chester Wheeler Campbell. Enter and a become engrossed in the story of a hit man for hire, drug wars, gangsters, good cops, bad cops, and court drama that erupted in the 1970's and lasted for almost two decades.

CHAPTER TWO

BRUSH WITH THE LAW

"This life of ours, this is a wonderful life. If you can get through life like this, hey, that's great. But it's very, very unpredictable. There are so many ways you can screw it up."
– "Big Paul" Castellano

OFFICER DAVID L. SAGE of the Keego Harbor Police Department could see the oncoming vehicle was travelling at a high rate of speed. Despite the temperature having hovered around 28 degrees, there was no snow to deal with and the street surface was relatively clear. Still, Orchard Lake Road was a narrow stretch requiring much safer speeds. Activity like this – occurring well after three in the morning - was certainly enough to strike the cop as more than a little suspicious.

Either playing chicken, loss of control, or just oblivious to other traffic, the sedan showed not a sign of slowing down in its northbound movement. Furthermore, from Sage's perspective, the oncoming automobile didn't make any attempt to steer clear of his patrol car. A frightful scenario was close to fruition.

As the two vehicles came dangerously close to front-end collision, Sage quickly took evasive action, maneuvering his car out of harms way. The mysterious sedan however took a sharp turn of the wheel, careening up the embankment and back onto the highway, again no signs of slowing down.

Officer Sage immediately turned his vehicle around and gave chase, following the perpetrator north on Orchard Lake Road, then westbound onto Indian Trail. He called in to report the chase; backup was on the way.

The picturesque area where this pursuit had now interrupted the tranquility is located just thirty miles northwest of Detroit. Close enough to be considered a suburb, with the city's amenities accessible, yet, Orchard Lake is distanced from the hustle, bustle and 'bad' elements found in major metropolitan areas. A buffer zone of beauty comprised of lakes, ponds and wooded areas fill the 908 square miles of Oakland County where the township is nestled. To the south, 8 Mile road serves as the southern border to Wayne County – home of the 'Motor City.' The usual sense of calm and normalcy Orchard Lake was perhaps accustomed to, well, that was abruptly changing on the night of February 6th, 1975 at 3:19 a.m.

Fortunately for Officer Sage though, the chase was short lived. Upon catching up with the suspect on Indian Trail, he observed a sedan, black 1975 Oldsmobile 98 Regency, pulled to the side of the road, with the apparent driver meandering around the outside of the vehicle. He parked directly behind the large 4 door, stepped out his patrol car and walked over to the driver to begin conversation. Sage questioned the driver, first trying to discover why the speeding car nearly collided with his patrol car. The driver had very little to say.

Jurisdiction was clearly in the hands of Orchard Lake police. Next to immediately arrive on scene were Corporal John Walsh, followed by Officer Edward Beyett of the Orchard Lake Police

Department. Each officer had responded, respectively, to Sage's backup call, and was in the vicinity at the time.

Soon after their appearance, another cop, Officer Bennett of nearby Sylvan Lake PD, pulled in front of the sedan. Standing together in the winter chill, four cops from three different police departments, plus one still-unidentified man adorned in s trendy clothes, and speaking with a slight attitude. The biting air that night was of no comparison to the unnerving truth that would come to the surface over the next several weeks.

CHAPTER THREE

ANATOMY OF A HIT MAN

"Class, that's the only thing that counts in life. Class. Without class and style, a man's a bum. He might as well be dead."
– Benjamin "Bugsy" Siegel

WHILE THE SUSPECT was being questioned at the rear of the Oldsmobile, initially by Officer Sage alone, Corporal Walsh and Officer Bennett began examining the car. According to Walsh's incident report, he could easily see a mess of objects scattered throughout the vehicle, because the driver's side door had been open the entire time allowing the dome to remain on.

"I then noticed several pieces of paper, notebooks, keys, money, and a wallet," he stated. "There was a lot of paper, books and other items scattered all over the car."

The most evident item to cause concern was first spotted by Sylvan Lake's Officer Bennett as he glanced in the vehicle from the front end. Through the windshield, Bennett spied a weapon in open view. A military style Colt .45 handgun rested on the driver's side seat. He called Walsh over to take a look. Illumina-

tion from the car's interior light revealed more suspicious elements. The curious officers took notice to one glaringly unlawful fact about this hefty piece of highly recognizable hardware.
Walsh saw the pistol was missing serial numbers. "Obliterated by
being drilled out," he declared of the weapon's condition, adding
the firearm was also, "loaded at the time I observed it."

Although police would sift more painstakingly through the
chaos of random items within the interior later, they were able
to locate the some identifying documents while at the scene,
including a wallet and the vehicle registration cards. The man
in question was finally identified as Chester Wheeler Campbell
from the 5000 block of Ivanhoe, Detroit Michigan.

As for the car, at first glimpse the Oldsmobile he was driving,
plate number 6599-HT, seemed much lived-in, perhaps that of
a travelling salesman. The general disorder of belongings strewn
about the car's interior could have been a circumstance of jostling
from the near collision. Or, conceivably, Campbell treated his
automobile like a second home. These were plausible theories,
until, as documents would subsequently confirm, Campbell was
positively not a salesman, at least in a traditional sense of the
vocation. The Olds? He didn't own it. The vehicle was a rental,
registered to a company called Rental Transportation, Inc. of
Ferndale Michigan.

Though obviously circumspect of the offender's character
based on the visible evidence, what these cops didn't conclusive-
ly know at the time was that Campbell happened to be much
more than a careless gun-toting driver on a wintery night. So,
what then was this Detroit man doing in the normally sedate
and peaceable Orchard Lake area? Carrying a loaded .45 with
no serial numbers? Although he was a new face to the suburban
police departments, Detroit and Michigan State Police had the

man in their sights for quite some time. Corporal Walsh and his team in Orchard Lake would find out soon enough with whom they were dealing.

Meanwhile, Walsh placed Campbell under arrest for carrying a concealed weapon in violation of statute 1983, and read him the Miranda rights. With no hesitation, Campbell responded directly, "I want to speak to my lawyer." The Corporal ceased questioning and placed the detainee in a patrol car. Walsh, Sage, and Bennett planned to escort Campbell to the Orchard Park Police Station while Officer Beyett arranged for the nearby Texaco station's Double K towing service to take the Oldsmobile to the city garage for lockdown.

Campbell whisked away in Walsh's car, headed for the police station. Beyett followed the tow truck to the city garage; the Sylvan Lake and Keego Harbor cops followed Walsh.

Thus far, the quartet of police officers collectively discovered the vehicle, which nearly crashed into Keego Harbor patrolman Sage's car, did not belong to the perpetrator, but a rental company rather. And, visibly from the suspect's identification and demeanor - he hailed from a tough section of Detroit and portrayed absolutely no intention of speaking to anyone but his attorney.

Chester Wheeler Campbell was taken into the Orchard Lake Police Department. Shortly after arrival, Walsh prepared to search Campbell's person again. Now, perhaps, they would discover a bit more about the tight-lipped man in custody.

Officer Beyett returned to the station quickly after he completed hold card #103 for the lock down of the Oldsmobile in the city garage. Upon his entrance, Beyett then stood witness to Corporal Walsh's pat down of Campbell. With every pocket emptied... more oddities were revealed.

Campbell kept an unusual number of loose, loaded cartridges

of assorted calibers on his person. He also carried a large sum of cash. A total of $3996 and some loose change were removed from Campbell's pockets. By now, suspicious wasn't even the word to describe the man they were detaining. Signs in the eyes of investigators, red flags blazing really, leaned increasingly towards the possibility that this guy's car was probably packed with a few more surprises.

So who was this man? Physically speaking, Orchard Park PD described Chester Wheeler Campbell as a black man weighing 200 lbs., standing at 5' 10", medium complexion, black hair and brown eyes. His rap sheet, as kept in State Police files, categorized Campbell in the 5'9" height range and 164 lbs., with numerous identifying marks about his frame. He had no recorded tattoos. All of the 'marks' were in fact scars. Chester Campbell's frame was marred with scars located upon his right shoulder, left shoulder, left knee, left wrist, and another on his neck. Files dating back to 1946 noted a set of three irregular scars on his elbow. As a teenager, he was also noted as having very good teeth, but by 1970 – on an arrest report from a narcotics raid at Chester's business – the notation expressed he now had "false teeth, upper and lower."

Some of his documentation noted him as being left-handed. One of his 'fake' forms of identification even listed, albeit vaguely, 'dark marks' located upon the wrist of his right hand and having hazel eyes.

Nevertheless, here was an individual with physical reminders of a life that was probably not so easy. Be it by choice, circumstance or both… Chester Wheeler Campbell was battle-scarred in more ways than one, emotionally blemished as well. (He would publicly say as much, or elude to at a later point, with haunting and dejected undertones – a bleak perception of himself.)

Chester's weight, like anyone else's, probably did in fact fluctuate over the years, but he intentionally described most of his physical characteristics in dissimilar ways – depending on the particular form of identification he was using at the time (Investigators would discover much more about his 'other' personas, and the purposes behind them in due time). He kept the world guessing on many fronts, including the specifics of his physical traits, by using a multitude of intentionally inconsistent phony forms of identification. His aliases included *John Burns*, hailing from Las Vegas Nevada and *Augustus Miller* of Cleveland Ohio (his preferred alter ego).

He unquestionably had a distinct presence though, regardless of who he was pretending to be at any given moment. He carried himself with an aura of authority, a level of confidence that so many of history's most infamous gangsters always seemed to assume.

He wore 17-1/2" in fitted dress shirts and a size extra large for his housecoat. His frame was a solid and unyielding, regardless of what weight and height he claimed to be. His eyes piercing, a mere glance from them showed he meant business. Chester Wheeler Campbell was equipped with an intimidating quality, and he was always dressed to impress.

Orchard Lake officers weren't looking to be spellbound; they were trying to figure out what this man was up to in their jurisdiction. They continued sifting through his pockets and the suspect was given a receipt for all the items cops removed from his person. The next step would be taking him to the county jail and wait for a judge to hear the charges.

CHAPTER FOUR

INVENTORY OF A HIT MAN

"The world says: "You have needs—satisfy them. You have as much right as the rich and the mighty. Don't hesitate to satisfy your needs; indeed, expand your needs and demand more." This is the worldly doctrine of today. And they believe that this is freedom. The result for the rich is isolation and suicide, for the poor, envy and murder."
— Fyodor Dostoevsky, The Brothers Karamazov

AFTER DELIVERING CAMPBELL to the Oakland County Jail, Orchard Lake officers Walsh and Beyett were responsible for completing the job of taking inventory in Campbell's car. So they headed to the city garage. Both officers took part in recording all the items scattered throughout the Oldsmobile. They meticulously logged everything, down to the little items like loose change and the number of matchbooks. Nothing was insignificant, and everything was to be inventoried *by the book*.

The search revealed handgun cartridges and shotgun shells, some in boxes, many randomly laying about the car interior. They found .45 caliber, .25 caliber, .32 caliber cartridges, and 12 gauge 00 buckshot as well. But Officer Beyett made a discovery that echoed Walsh's major find at the original crime scene on Indian Trail.

"I found a loaded pistol on the floor in front of the driver's seat," said Beyett, "with the serial number obliterated by being drilled out."

The gun Beyett uncovered was a Belgium Dictator, semi automatic, 6.35mm (.25ACP), with a five round clip. This particular series of firearms was manufactured from 1909 through 1925 by arms maker Societe Anonyme Des Fabriques d'Armes, Reunies. The gun was basically a vintage piece, but certainly still in potentially deadly working condition; old and virtually impossible to trace.

Now the cops had discovered two loaded handguns, each weapon showing obvious signs of tampering to conceal the origin. Then, Walsh found an envelope containing a plastic bottle, which contained a white powdery substance. In observing Walsh's discovery, Beyett made further notes, adding, "Also in the white envelope were two small yellow envelopes containing a white powdery substance." The smaller envelopes would prove conclusive to the officer's suspicions of narcotics, but unbeknownst to the investigators - also serve as a catalyst for Campbell's forthcoming personal fury against Corporal Walsh.

Without a warrant, the police could not legally begin a full examination of the trunk contents, but the discovery of the buckshot shell within the car's interior area absolutely struck a chord with Walsh as much if not more than the suspected drug find. They found cartridges matching both the weapons discovered already in the car's interior, but not the type of gun that would utilize a Remington 12-gauge shell. So the trunk was popped open and Walsh simply 'felt' around a loose covering of blankets and plastic. With his hand he traced something beneath the layers and commented to Beyett, "It feels like it could be a gun."

The trunk was closed at that point. Following the rule of law, cops would have to get a search warrant before continuing onward to the impounded Oldsmobile's secrets. So while Chester Wheeler Campbell remained locked up in Oakland County jail, police knew the next step was a visit to the prosecutor to secure a warrant. They had to find out what secrets resided within the trunk of the 98 Oldsmobile. If that search revealed darker surprises, then Campbell's home was surely next on the investigation list.

First things first though, and the officers took the inventory of items back to the office. Weapons and ammunition were locked in the vault. Then Officer Beyett took charge of the 'envelopes' found in Campbell's rental car and headed to the Michigan State Police Crime Detection Laboratory in Warren. Beyett delivered the suspect items to Mr. Gary Backos of the lab at 8:30 a.m. on February 6th. Backos listed the items received as; one opened envelope containing a coin envelope with an off-white powder, a coin envelope with a few round white tablets, and a coin envelope with a plastic bag containing a white granular substance. Also, a plastic vial with a white granular substance.

Two hours later, Backos had news to share. He told Beyett of his findings regarding the 'powdery white substances' contained in the envelopes. "Mr. Backos informed me that the substance in one of the small yellow envelopes contained heroin," said Beyett, "a narcotic listed under Schedule 1 of the Controlled Substances Act."

With the findings positive for heroin, he quickly took the information to the Oakland County Prosecutor's office to secure a felony warrant. Corporal Walsh arrived as well. He then discussed the issue of obtaining a warrant to search Campbell's trunk with Assistant Prosecutor Richard Thompson. Thompson concurred, and had Walsh fill out the affidavit for the search warrant. As the 'affiant' for the warrant, Walsh stated the search of the Oldsmobile trunk area was for a "12 gauge shotgun, and any controlled substances, including heroin and Phencyclidine, also known as PCP."

Also mentioned in the request for a search warrant was Walsh's conversation with an officer from Detroit – closely familiar with Campbell's reputation. Walsh had spoken with Alfred James of the Internal Affairs Division, Section 318, just prior to requesting the warrant. James was familiar with the mysterious man Orchard Lake had arrested. James told Walsh that Campbell "Was known to carry and use a shotgun" and was wanted on an outstanding bench warrant for drugs. Furthermore, James relayed to Walsh that Campbell was wanted on six counts of conspiracy in Wayne County. Essentially the most alarming piece of information Alfred James and other Detroit cops offered to Walsh had to do with Chester Wheeler Campbell's chosen profession. It was now quite clear: a man with a very dangerous reputation in neighboring Wayne County had visited the area known as Orchard Lake!

Walsh was apparently confident that Campbell was in possession of PCP. Therefore the sworn affidavit's listing of PCP (known on the street as "Angel Dust") is important because, within months, Chester Wheeler Campbell would use this information in an attempt to legally maneuver himself out of trouble, and get some revenge. Technically, the crime lab did not state findings of any angel dust in the results of the tests conducted on the 'envelopes' found in Campbell's car. The incarcerated hit man would try to obtain some payback in the following months.

For now though, Chester Wheeler Campbell's secrets from the trunk were going to be unveiled. Walsh and Beyett were armed with a warrant to search, and they expected to find, at the very least, a weapon to match the buckshot shells they had in the evidence vault back at the station.

Walsh and Beyett drove back to the city garage and began executing the search at 2:15 p.m. This had already become one of the longest days of their respective police careers, in terms of hours and more importantly the subject of the work. Working non-stop since three-thirty in the morning, the police were determined to uncover everything possible regarding Chester Wheeler Campbell. This case was unusual for Orchard Lake; ominous revelations with every hour that passed.

Corporal John Walsh popped open the trunk of Campbell's rented Oldsmobile. He lifted the blanket covering, which revealed the first of several secrets.

"I found a Winchester rifle, Model 94, .44 magnum, lever action, serial number 9169," Walsh stated, adding the weapon, "was wrapped in a brown plastic bag."

He then removed a small attaché case from the trunk. This find was particularly eerie. Housed inside the case was a sawn-off shotgun – a weapon that matched the loaded 00 buckshot they found in the vehicle interior earlier that morning.

Walsh examined the gun, stating it was "A Winchester shotgun, Model 97, 12 gauge, Serial number 1017609."

This particular shotgun, also known as a "trench gun" for it's common military use, was a popular weapon for many decades. Reliable and powerful in its standard barrel length of 30", but Chester's was illegally modified to half that size. Sawed down to a barrel length of a mere fifteen inches, and the stock fashioned into a pistol grip shape, there are really only two reasons for such modifications: concealment and maneuverability. The gun found was only 27-1/2" overall, easily hidden in the attaché case and capable of deadly force in quick or confined circumstances.

Campbell also had a police scanner, shoulder holsters for the handguns, numerous scrapbooks filled with newspaper clipping and something even more highly unusual – copies of Grand Jury transcripts. Transcripts of this nature are highly sensitive and positively not for the public; Campbell could never have been in possession of these unless he had connections.

Walsh and Beyett's final discovery was, however, the most detailed, revealing and frightening of all. It was the sort of find that truly put Chester's name in newspaper headlines – and the collective conscious of Greater Detroit's police, judges, and prosecutors. Notebooks. Orchard Lake officers didn't realize the importance of these notebooks' contents just yet, but within days of the discovery... the true purpose of Chester Wheeler Campbell would come to light. Within weeks, the media was having a field day with the story because the tale was unfolding like a movie plot only found in a Hollywood script. This was a very real situation though and cops weren't taking any chances while investigating Mr. Chester Wheeler Campbell.

After he was lodged at the Oakland County Jail earlier in the morning of February 6th, Campbell was initially booked on two counts of carrying a concealed weapon, plus the drug charge for possession of heroin. In court the next day, Judge Cifelli set Campbell's bond at $5000. Chester Campbell, always-in guardianship of a lot of cash, still wasn't leaving the jail anytime soon for bond set at a mere five grand.

Corporal John Walsh took the guns to the Regional Crime Detection Laboratory on February 7th and submitted them to Detective Sgt. Robert J. Cameron for examination. The result of finger print tests found Campbell's right hand print on the barrel of the .44 magnum rifle. His left hand print was identified on the stock of the same weapon. All of the guns were put through ballistics tests. The lab's findings on all the confiscated firearms were as follows:

"Test shots from the firearm are not identifiable with any open shooting cases on file at this Michigan State Police Scientific Laboratory."

The 44. Magnum rifle however was turned over to the Firearms Identification Unit after it was discovered this particular weapon was on record as being stolen. The sawn-off 12-gauge shotgun was handed over to Officer Beyett, it was noted as being either 'not registered' or 'stolen.'

On February 8th, Judge Ingraham set the bond $100,000 in light of the 'trunk' discovery made by Orchard Lake police. The long rife in the trunk was not the most detrimental issue (notwithstanding the fact a convicted felon is not permitted to own firearms at all and this weapon was stolen), but the sawn-off shotgun most certainly was, so a fourth count of Carrying a Concealed Weapon was immediately added. Campbell also went before Judge Alice Gilbert. His bond would again be upped another $100,000 before all was said and done. Judges Ingraham and Gilbert, in particular, would both be added to the growing list of people that infuriated Chester.

Judge Gilbert remembers Chester Campbell very clearly. "The first time he appeared," she says, "he had a very expensive pair of snakeskin or alligator shoes. Really dressed expensively, maybe not in the best of tastes, but in his taste. Thereafter, I don't know what happened to the shoes but they disappeared by the time he went to trial."

Gilbert served as Judge for forty-two years, and had more than a few memorable cases brought before her over that lengthy span. Chester's was certainly one of those remarkable and unforgettable characters. "It was just a normal arraignment on one charge," she adds, "but it's what happened subsequently that was the issue. He had three additional charges and that's when the issue of the Grand Jury proceedings found in his trunk, along with other weapons, came up. The interesting thing, he had a murder warrant but hid out for three years and here he was – a black man living in a white community, the suburbs of Detroit. I assume he was here the whole time, but nobody thought much of it."

Relating to all the incredible, illegal, legal and even mundane items found in Campbell's car, and in addition to the impression he was leaving on all those who encountered him- much can be derived about otherwise 'cagey' individuals from their personal effects. Theories, facts and conjecture all intermingle, and even if certain things aren't necessarily evidence, that doesn't mean one can't figure out a lot of what someone's intentions might be.

Chester Wheeler Campbell kept in the car and on his person quite an array of such possessions. These policemen couldn't have any idea the magnitude of the story to unfold over the following months, but they quickly began to understand they were not dealing with a typical criminal offender.

Beyond his physical features and the suspicious objects he carried (both on his person and in his vehicle) – much can be derived about Campbell from his everyday personal belongings.

The police officers meticulously recorded every single item – down to the brand of shaving kit – which Campbell kept in the vehicle. Taken at face value, many of the recorded objects could be found on any law-abiding citizen during that era. It was 1975, a time when plaid, animal prints, wide ties, double-knit slacks and other wild patterns were still, to some degree, en vogue. Chester had hip taste in fashion, an obvious concern for appearance, and definitely a regimen for personal hygiene. Campbell could look the part of an average everyday guy, and conversely, he was well prepared to fit the stereotypical image of a gangster. He was as practiced at comfortably hanging out with a tough West Detroit crowd as he was making deals with downtown mob types.

He liked the music of the late Otis Redding, and apparently took good care of that technological wonder– the 8-track player – as supported by the Ampex brand cleaner tapes. The forty-four year old was concerned about graying hair and he liked fresh breath and smooth skin.

He had a taste for Scotch, and over the counter pain relievers. Nasal decongestants, headache relief and ear wax removal – Campbell kept backups of each. Money, as demonstrated by the large amounts he kept scattered throughout the car and on his person, was evidently not an object. Cash was found in the glove box, behind the seats, and simply 'laying' about the floor. He absolutely enjoyed the finer things, among them the cars, clothes, a gold signet pinky ring, and even the types of firearms he had amassed.

The inventory of items dispersed throughout the Oldsmobile read like a shopping list of everyday necessities, with a distinct twist of the wicked. A total of one hundred different items were scattered throughout the car, each thoroughly catalogued by police.

For the basics of daily provisions, Campbell was definitely on top of maintaining a clean appearance and battling skin imperfections. Cocoa butter, breath mints, astringent, several variations of Aramis brand face products and the ever-popular Wilkinson shaving kit, among the items logged by investigators. He kept a travel iron, de-icer and a multitude of pills for sinus relief.

He preferred Zizanie and Faberge colognes for himself, Chantilly perfume for the ladies. Chester Wheeler Campbell came prepared for virtually any situation, and being at his personal best

– cleanliness and appearance especially was top priority. From car deodorizers to foot powder, Campbell was never short on the products necessary to keep him on top of his game.

Beyond the hygiene and vanity products, which certainly gave investigators a better idea of the type of person their suspect was, Campbell's business related inventory was what police were most interested in. There were also numerous packages of flash bars and film for the Polaroid SX-70 Land Camera. A hot item in 1975 for consumers in general, this model spit out the 'instant' picture. Campbell considered the camera an absolute necessity. Infiltration, eavesdropping and intelligence gathering also required being able to 'watch' from a distance. Of course he had a good set of binoculars: Tasco Model 108, 7x-15x-35mm.

He transported; effectively, everything one would require for any situation, at a moments notice, all packed into attaché cases, paper bags and cloth bags. That which wasn't tucked away… was scattered throughout every nook and cranny of the Oldsmobile 98.

Looking back upon the diversity and jumbled state of items on his person and in the rental car, the question is raised: Was Chester Wheeler Campbell a 'disorganized' guy? Or, as noted earlier, perhaps the disarray was a natural result of the near miss accident dispersing his belongings about? Was he just a walking dichotomy; organized chaos?

Street legends regarding his highly sought after talents would suggest the latter scenario, if any. Campbell was rumored to receive hit fees upwards of, possibly, ten thousand dollars, and both the mob and drug lords alike employed his services.

"Chester Campbell was versed at being able to be flexible between factions," organized crime historian Scott M. Burnstein adds. "He didn't work directly under any of them, but kind of freelance, back and forth between Italians and blacks. He was considered a very qualified strong arm."

As such, an otherwise 'messy' individual would most likely not have been an ideal candidate for professional assassin, let alone command such high remuneration for dealing death and dope. Maybe, just maybe, Chester was a little cluttered, but certainly not sloppy.

Chester was both street smart and book smart . He was also an avid reader, and a card-carrying member of the Detroit Public Library in fact. A habit no doubt picked up while serving over thirteen years in a penitentiary, with very little else to do, Chester voraciously consumed many types of literary materials. He not only read a lot, he usually tried to apply, wherever applicable in his dynamic and layered lifestyle, much of what he absorbed from each chosen selection.

Several books of considerable significance were found scattered amongst his belongings in the Oldsmobile. From looking at each title documented in his possession... a few theories regarding his possible *ulterior motives*, or mindset could be considered. The literary materials discovered by Orchard Park P.D. included selections that are, practically, testaments to Campbell's interest and thought process.

The book entitled *Hypnotism* by Walter Brown Gibson was marked item #41 on the *Tabulation Pursuant to Search Warrant* (a total of 100 individual entries of seized property were listed and submitted as evidence). Released in 1970, this was a short examination of the history and modern use and abuse of hypnotism. The author, Gibson, was actually best known as a magician and his work with the comic book character *The Shadow*.

Adding to Campbell's interest in the fine art of manipulation, he also had a hardcover copy of *Proof, Persuasion and Cross-Ex-*

amination by author Louis E Schwartz. Again, a title that speaks for itself in terms of subject matter – and what the reader would hope to glean from its pages. Campbell thoroughly enjoyed, felt compelled really, to learn everything he could – specifically regarding the process of the American legal system.

Coming in at #42 was a fourth-edition printing of *Real Estate Investments*. Unless Campbell was considering a drastic career change, this selection seems to suggest he was likely looking for ways to 'launder' the noticeably large amounts of cash he kept stuffed in virtually every corner of his car, home and person. Investigators quickly learned, however, that Chester actually owned and had financial interest in several properties around West Detroit, various businesses. Although he was making legitimate money through these ventures, he would also logically have to find a way to 'clean' the drug money as well – the find seemed to point that direction.

Orchard Lake police also discovered a paperback copy of author Jon Palmer's provocative first novel, released in 1973, called *House Full of Brothers*. A work of fiction, but taking on a real social issue of the time, Palmer's tale follows the struggles of black man's college and post-college life – with a twist. From the book's description: *"Steven Walls blew into L.A. from Omaha seeking his California Dream: membership in a black fraternity, an education, a prestigious job---and a white woman. That's what it took to make it in the white man's world, Steven thought. And that's exactly what he got---until he was booked for a bank robbery and murder he didn't commit, and Walls came tumbling down."*

And then there was the book called *Dealer*. Written by Richard Woodley, it was recorded as the sixty-third item found in Campbell's vehicle. Originally published as a hardcover in 1971;

Chester's version was the 1972 paperback print. Subtitled *Portrait of a Cocaine Merchant*, Woodley's examination of the drug world, featured a very 'Superfly*esque*' photo on the cover and a reviewer's blurb calling it "An authentic glimpse into a bizarre scene." The book was, for the time period, considered quite controversial, yet incredibly accurate and enlightening in its documentation of a New York drug dealer's daily routine.

Chester was already fully immersed in a genuine underworld scene. A book of this nature could have served as a guide, some inspiration or simply as a source of glorification. Campbell now had his own reputation on the streets and in police files. His ego was pumped by it all. Image and reference purposes were both very likely reasons behind his interest in this title.

Campbell also had intricate and expensive "spy" equipment in the car. Surveillance, counter-surveillance... he was adept in the art and science of espionage. Corporal John Walsh and patrolman Edward Beyett found what it commonly called a "bug" in the vehicle. Among the multitude of random papers they sifted through, the officers removed receipts for even more equipment and supplies of this nature. Considering the time period, and the cost of having his car outfitted with spy gadgets... he spared no expense. Chester Wheeler Campbell knew what to buy, how to use it, and of course... where to get the best of the best.

Campbell frequented, via mail order, an electronics company based in Florida. The R.B. Clifton Company was once a popular supply house for civilians seeking surveillance gear. Among the accessories Campbell had receipts for – beepers, receivers, cables, antennas and fittings to mount the equipment to a vehicle dashboard. He was essentially retrofitting a vehicle as though he were a character straight out of a James Bond movie.

Though the contents were still in the box when cops searched his car, what Chester Campbell was planning, thanks to the high-end implements he was planning to install, included the ability to track others and, perhaps even more importantly, making sure the police and enemies weren't tracking him. He even made sure his purchases were not shipped to his own home. He used the address of a nearby joint called Skeeter's Club for his spy gear packages and paid with cashier's checks. Interestingly, Campbell had proprietary interest in Skeeter's Club, among other West Detroit assets where he would conduct 'business' of one sort or another.

Still, it was Chester's other 'day' job that was the most unusual, ironic, and in a bizarre way – not that surprising really. There was evidence found to suggest his girlfriend actually, and legitimately, employed him, but the scenario was just as strange as every other piece of evidence being uncovered regarding his life and career path. Police would look further into this relationship over the coming weeks.

On February 11th, Campbell, strolled through the halls of the 48th District court in Bloomfield, escorted by officers and detectives. Wearing a chic animal print jacket, open collar white shirt, he observed his surroundings with a pursed lips and a defiant glare. Without access to his grooming accessories, Chester's hair was streaking with more grays, but he carried himself with a distinguished look regardless.

He wouldn't be able to 'primp' himself anytime soon. The law wasn't finished upping his bond. In fact, by now, they had no intention of allowing the alleged hit man to leave the confines of a cell. By the time presiding judges were through with him, his bond reached $400,000 – one hundred thousand per each count. He was beyond livid, and secured two reliable stalwarts of his character to defend and fight for his bond.

CHAPTER FIVE

HISTORY OF A HIT MAN

*"Where justice is denied, where poverty is enforced, where igno-
rance prevails, and where any one class is made to feel that society is
an organized conspiracy to oppress, rob and degrade them, neither
persons nor property will be safe."*
- Frederick Douglass

TO **UNDERSTAND A** man like Chester Wheeler Campbell
is to examine the environment he spent much of his
life immersed in. What is known of his past, Campbell
was a Michigan native, born and raised in Detroit. December
4, 1930 is when he came into this world, the fourth of six children. Chester was named after his father, who had died by the
time *junior* was in second grade. His mother Margaret originally
hailed from Georgia, but joined her husband, a Louisiana native,
to find a better life in the north – just as many southern African
Americans had done during the early twentieth century. As fate
would have it though, the widowed Margaret Campbell was left
to care for the six children on her own, in an apartment building
that housed three other families, on a section of Hague Street
that is now comprised of empty lots and freeway.

Although by some accounts greater Detroit was considered

a magnificent huge melting pot of ethnic groups, the cold hard truth was that racial inequality and tension ran deep in the city. Growing up in such a divided period of time certainly made options limited or more difficult to realize, especially for young blacks.

It was a critical time in history, not just for Detroit but the whole country. The Great Depression hammered the entire nation's financial makeup, and prohibition was still in effect, albeit unsuccessfully keeping liquor illegal and out of the hands of the general public. Basically, while the legitimate folks of every ethnic and cultural background were struggling just to get by... mobsters in the Motor City, just like in other major cities, were of the very few groups still raking in the dough.

Statistically, during the years between 1910 and 1930, the African American population of Detroit grew 1991%. To make a comparison of this growth, Cleveland was the next closest coming in at a 751% increase of blacks between those same years.

Oppression and segregation (which reared its ugly head in numerous forms, including real estate 'red lines' and job discrimination) of the many 'southern' blacks that moved north during those years would culminate in riotous backlash on more than one occasion (most notably 1967). Suffice to say Chester Wheeler Campbell wasn't exactly born into a time or place that was very welcoming to people of such skin tone. When the promise of a better life appeared so attainable, for so many seeking jobs in the auto industry, yet realistically became very much out of reach, it is no wonder why some people strayed into the criminal underworld. Right or wrong – it was survival of the fittest.

Whatever underlying issues truly contributed to creating a future assassin may never be fully known, and certainly not excused. However, it was clear by the mid 1940's, the law and

Chester already met and weren't exactly getting along well.

Chester Wheeler Campbell managed to make it to secondary school, but not much further. He graduated the ninth grade before he and the law met on unpleasant terms. He had taken to thievery as an after school activity, and it caught up with him, thus ending his chances with any further formal education.

The teenager was arrested in September of 1946 for one count of burglary. He and three other fifteen and sixteen year old boys were caught breaking into a drug store. By February of 1947 – his first conviction was levied from that infraction. The sentence was from one to 15 years. Released in relatively short time, he ran right back to a life of petty theft. Chester's criminal record was gaining considerable momentum.

Just three years following his first criminal conviction, Detroit police nailed Campbell for felony breaking and entering, but the details of what transpired showed young Campbell was habitually robbing the same location – a local drug store in close proximity to the barber and beauty shop he was working as a porter for. The F & F Drug Company was missing money on a regular basis, taken right out of the cash register. Julius Glatter, the co-owner reported the repeated thefts to police in February 1950. Detectives decided to stake the store out since it appeared the thefts were occurring regularly. On March 11, at 7:50 in the morning, two Detroit cops, Sgt. Simmons and Detective Christy, caught Chester Campbell climbing through a skylight shared by both the drug store and the beauty shop where he worked. He was arrested, booked and sentenced a month later to ten months to five years term.

Again he left the confines of a cell in short order. However, in 1955, he upped the ante, graduating to the most serious of crimes. At 5 p.m., July 1st, Chester and two accomplices set out to shake down a known numbers joint. It was a loosely planned scheme to rob the gambling operation located on Lawton Street in West Detroit. Shortly after arrival, he and his cohorts carried out a general shakedown of the place, but encountered resistance from a man named Luther Mixon while trying to conclude their heist. In the course of just a few moments and over a brief exchange of threats, Mixon was shot dead and the trio of would-be robbers fled the scene.

The following day, Chester and an associate – Walter Greene – were hanging outside a store when a Detroit police officer recognized Campbell. The officer had recognized Campbell as a suspect in a robbery the month before. He arrested both men and confiscated a .38 caliber revolver, a pair of blue women's silk gloves and a money clip with $100 in cash. An odd assortment of items indeed, but the arresting officer was totally unaware Chester had committed his first murder the evening prior.

Chester Campbell maneuvered his way around the arrest and succeeded in maintaining a low profile for almost a month before police finally tracked him down again. On July 27 he was arrested on one count of homicide, and subsequently brought to trial in January 1956. Five witnesses testified against him as Judge Krauss presided. A jury found him guilty on January 12th. Seven days later, the judge sentenced him. The crime of murder was given a life sentence; this time at least, he would spend many years behind bars.

While confined in Michigan's oldest and largest penitentiary, Michigan State Prison (aka Jackson State Prison) – Chester learned not only how the structure of law really worked, but also in what way he could work it right back for his own benefit. He was familiar with the inner workings of the prison; he'd been there before. For this offense though, he was dealt thirteen years of confinement, which he used to study and contemplate a future outside the lines of law and order. He was not seeking rehabilitation, although an education was indeed on his agenda. Campbell wasn't interested in degrees or diplomas. He was however learning the intricacies of criminal law, the process, the system, and how to control it. The art and science of manipulation was, especially, something Campbell would employ throughout the rest of his life, both outside and inside the prison system.

CHAPTER SIX

WHEN A GOOD COP GOES BAD

*"In each of us, two natures are at war – the good and the evil.
All our lives the fight goes on between them, and one of them must
conquer. But in our own hands lies the power to choose – what we
want most to be we are."*
- **Robert Louis Stevenson**

Heroin (and cocaine to a lesser degree) was the source of very big business for both the black and Italian factions of Detroit's underworld, particularly by the end of the 1960's. Of course illicit drugs such as marijuana, various pills, and psychedelics were popular, but the 'smack' was where big money came into the hands of traffickers and dealers. Pure heroin powder would be cut with other substances before it was street ready. In stark contrast to the frighteningly high contemporary levels of purity (up to 90% is not uncommon for addicts to obtain today), the heroin product reaching users in the 1950's and 1960's was between ten and twenty percent pure.

While Chester Wheeler Campbell was serving out his 1956 murder conviction, the city was unquestionably in the midst of an even larger scale drug influx. Some former middle class sections of Detroit had become home to hundreds of addicts, and the race issue was truly ushering in a very real battleground between police and minorities.

Furthermore, a swing in the organized crime ruling class, as it pertained to narcotics trafficking specifically, was taking place. This shift essentially went hand in hand with the already and ever-present racial divide that existed for decades.

"From 1931 to 1970, forty years, the Italians were the only ballgame in town," says organized crime historian Scott M. Burnstein. "There was virtually no violence, when you put it in relative terms to other cities where there were faction wars taking place. Detroit was relatively peaceful, or factions co-existed."

To see how this 'shift' in narcotic dealing evolved, a look back to the end of prohibition is a good starting point. The Jewish element of organized crime – which essentially ran a large part of Detroit's bootlegging business during the roaring twenties, with a very violent resolve, began to dwindle following the Volstead Act's repeal. Not entirely gone, but for the most part the notorious Purple Gang was in decline by the early 1930's.

Partially, the reason was simply economic changes and many younger Jews entering the legitimate business routes. Others simply assimilated back into legitimate society. This subtle but important change in Detroit was also taking place in New York. There was absolutely still a Jewish faction for many decades to come, but on a larger scale things had transferred to the Italian mob that more than happily filled in Detroit's underworld gaps.

The Mafia grabbed up gambling, union and drug rackets, taking ultimate control of the latter. "Basically," Burnstein explains of the mob's control, "You could say it was all the mob, from prohibition to 1967, when the riots erupted, which was another watershed moment in the city history."

But that didn't mean 'exclusivity' in such swindles. The illegal drug trade that began to prosper in the inner city especially, well, that was carried out by the new era of African-American gangsters – under the guise of Italian bosses (for the moment).

One individual in particular, a highly regarded former narcotics cop, cast a shadow over Detroit's finest, effectively showing just how tempting the drug game could be even for highly decorated lawmen. His name was Henry Marzette, a black man who, for a little while at least, was viewed as a truly shining star of police work.

During the early through mid 1950's, Marzette and his partner William Frank made headlines on more than one occasion for their spectacular dope ring busts, delivering crushing blows to the city's worst drug offenders, particularly those in the heroin business. One of the most amazing adventures the veteran cop Frank and his protégé Marzette had undertaken – a covert jailhouse investigation.

A few years before a young Chester Wheeler Campbell was sent to prison for murder, the twenty-six year old Marzette was being lauded for amazing police work. It was 1953 and only a year on the force, the fearless young cop daringly went inside prison walls disguised as a 'bum' to infiltrate and root out a drug conspiracy. On a tip, cops decided to investigate alleged opiate trafficking inside the prison. The narcotics detail devised the successful plan after one of the ring's members, fifty-seven year old Eugene Crowley, told authorities he, "wanted to get out from under it." Marzette, and an informant, were processed into the prison, carrying marked bills.

Two brothers, Stephen and William Nawrocki, had been supplying the drugs from the outside to their twenty-seven year old brother Peter, who was incarcerated in the Detroit House of Correction. Peter, with the help of fellow conspirators, then distributed the dope to other inmates, primarily on the grounds of the detention center's 'farm', which housed about 600 inmates. How the operation worked, as authorities uncovered thanks to Marzette's efforts, the prisoners who sought narcotics wore the initials 'A.F.' on their shirts to signify such desire.

Under William Frank's tutelage, Henry Marzette successfully subverted the narcotics ring over several days spent undercover and came out with honors. Five prisoners were charged, and four of those were placed in solitary confinement after the bust. "It was the first time I had been on anything that big," Marzette told the press, "But Frank schooled me."

Along with mentor William Frank (who chalked up his sixth departmental citation for excellence), Marzette received one for "effort and ingenuity", also earning the nickname "Lucky" immediately following the bust.

As is often the case, when one form of racket exists – there are usually others, so therefore it wasn't long before Detroit investigators also found that opiates were not the only contraband being smuggled into the Detroit House of Correction. "Women and Liquor," are what the prosecutor said was also being brought in for inmates. The discovery of booze and prostitutes came within days of Henry Marzette's incredible undercover drug sting.

Marzette and Frank were the cream of the crop, raising the bar for police work in Detroit. The duo continued to make big drug busts for another three years. In 1954 the pair was responsible for cracking another large ring. At the time, a large percentage of heroin was entering Detroit via traffickers from New York. After the arrest of one such major dealer, the dynamic pair of superstar cops got wind of a 'replacement' on his way to re-establish the drug route between the two major cities.

Marzette and Frank waited for three weeks, following a solid tip, for a man named Harold Bunce to make his move. The officers eventually spotted and tailed a Cadillac driving around town that belonged to the jailed drug boss Richard Boyd. They stopped the car and arrested Bunce, along with a woman named Kae Alexander. Henry Marzette and William Frank made national headlines once again. They remarked to the media that they successfully broke the ring, busting the replacement kingpin and seizing an ounce of pure heroin, which was worth about $15,000 on the street once it was cut and packaged.

The glory wasn't going to last much longer though. By the tail end of the decade, William Frank, Henry Marzette and over two-dozen others, including men and women from both the Motor City and Cleveland, were arraigned on corruption charges themselves. Yes, they too were dealing narcotics, and in March 1956 – the racket was busted, making newspaper headlines across the nation in a much different manner than the cops were used to. An example, such as the one from the March 19th, 1956 edition Press-Telegram in Long Beach, California, said it all – **"Police Hero, Protégé Arrested in Roundup..."**

Ultimately, they were 'schooled' in the tactics of drug distribution, yet now found themselves in cuffs. They had the knowledge and contacts drawn from the intimate experience only narcotics police work could provide. The lure of money, and a first-hand comprehension of how to do and not do business in narcotics, convinced these once-star players to switch teams.

Detroit and Cleveland narcotics investigators had been watching them very closely, for over four months. In all, over twenty people were arrested in the bust. At least two, including Marzette and Frank, were cops.

Cleveland authorities were so determined to keep the investigation on track that several officials publicly lashed out at the press. In fear of having cases derailed by too much media coverage, lips were sealed on arrest details, but sharp tongues let loose on the newspaper reporters.

"I'm working for the country," declared Raymond Ripberger of the Treasury Department, narcotics bureau, "Not the newspapers."

Ripberger went on to tell the crowd of impatient reporters to go to Detroit, as he wasn't in any mood or position to discuss the ongoing investigation in Cleveland. "We don't have to stop in the middle of an investigation to make an announcement," he snapped.

Marzette and Frank were brought up on conspiracy charges, and off to prison they went. In similar fashion to the group they busted in the prison ring, the disgraced cops were found not only be involved in drug dealing, but also suspected connection with prostitution rackets.

Their boss, Inspector Russell McCarty, believed the group was even more expansive and felt additional people would be arrested before all was said and done. At the time of Frank and Marzette's fall from grace, McCarty estimated around "2400 addicts in the city." The now-suspended cops and their cohorts were inexplicably behind the supply that served many of those addicts with their 'fix'. How much dope did investigators think the pair was distributing? U.S. Attorney Fred Kaess told the press he believed the operation was supplying between sixty and seventy percent of the heroin that entered Detroit. Kaess also held, albeit incorrectly, that taking down Marzette and Frank was, "instrumental in stamping out a substantial supply of narcotics brought into this area."

This was certainly positive thinking, but the reality of the situation reached far beyond the two jailed cops. Again, the Italian mob was responsible for bringing the entire heroin supply into the city. The blacks were often couriers or distributing from there. This was going to change in due time, but for the moment it seemed investigators were winning some battles – yet still not fighting the actual war.

Somehow Henry Marzette and William Frank made it back onto the streets in very short time. In the fall of 1957 the cops turned convicts had been busy, back to the drug business as outlaws. When authorities broke up yet another New York narcotics pipeline, which included routes to Detroit, Henry Marzette, William Frank, along with Clarence Wilson (also a former cop) were taken into custody. The three ex-police were part of sixty-two-person roundup that officials considered part of a multi-million dollar narcotics trafficking operation.

The twists and turns of Marzette's story continued. Once the indictment was unsealed, it was revealed that all three former cops were not named as defendants after all. Oddly, they were considered "co-conspirators" in what was being called a seven-year running, twenty million dollar per year, multi-state narcotics ring. In other words, the three were among those considered 'lesser', albeit important actors involved in the ring.

This revelation gained some of the media's attention. Speculation began to circulate that Marzette and company most likely provided at least some form of 'assistance' to authorities during the investigation process. Such insinuations, in the world of crime, are often met with deadly resolve. If the whispers of 'informer' or 'rat' were in the air, amazingly it didn't end up having much negative effect on Henry Marzette's future in the criminal world.

Marzette had adapted fairly well to the transition from cop to convict. Prison life was not difficult, and while incarcerated, Marzette had been rumored to even work some 'enforcement' for mafia factions. He was always making moves for a life of crime to unfold yet again after his eventual release, forever an outlaw from that moment on.

Marzette returned to the free world in the earlier 1960's, virtually unnoticed by the press, and went straight back to work in Detroit's escalating dope game. This time, however, his return would be on a much grander scale. Although his post-prison life is shrouded in plenty of mystery (the major Detroit media seemed largely disinterested in covering the reemergence of this dishonored cop at the time), he was said to be quite a sharp dresser, enjoyed the finer things in life and commanded a loyal following. Furthermore, he was virtually unimpeded by any law enforcement entities in the West Detroit area. He was called a "Gorilla Pimp" on the seedy streets for his reputation of forcibly stripping local pimps of their prostitutes and putting them to work for his own racket. But drugs were the moneymakers, and he watched closely over the years, taking mental notes on just how profitable the heroin trade was for the Italian mob.

Henry Marzette can also be credited with launching a departure of sorts, one whereby many black drug traffickers eventually agreed to bypass the mafia-controlled drug pipelines. Heroin importation by traffickers, and subsequent abuse by users was rising steadily year-by-year since Marzette's arrest in 1956. By the late 1960's, the opiate had become a huge source of cash for criminals.

Scott Burnstein explains, "At a certain point in the late 60's he decided to circumvent the Italians. He wanted independence for the black dealers."

Henry Marzette was rumored to have, by 1970, already set up parcels of land in the Caribbean, specifically Jamaica, for cultivation of Opium Poppy plants – the first step in heroin production.

He was known to make frequent trips to the island. This was a bold business move indeed, but also very savvy. Marzette was essentially building the foundation to bypass not only the Detroit mafia, but also the entire established network of 'known' sources. While black gangsters from the East Coast, such as Frank "Black Caesar" Matthews, were making incredible headway in their own right, establishing deals within the infamous mafia operated "French Connection" and others were getting supplied directly from Southeast Asia from savvy traffickers like Ike "Sergeant Smack" Atkinson, Henry Marzette was trying to build his own empire – from production to distribution. What was occurring in Detroit – the growing independence of black gangsters from the Mafia's grasp – also came to fruition in other major cities beginning in the late 1960's. Taking away the heroin trade from the mob on a rapidly spreading national level... it was a heavy blow to every Mafia crime family.

CHAPTER SEVEN

RIOT AND REVOLT

"The excessive increase of anything causes a reaction in the opposite direction."
- **Plato**

HENRY MARZETTE WAS a true kingpin of the heroin trade, tailored from head to toe, virtually untouchable, and determined to break from the past. His proactive measures to free himself from the heavy hand of mafia drug traffickers was applauded by some and challenged by others. A ripple in the establishment was quickly becoming a giant chasm. This was a polarizing situation that mirrored issues present in the lives of law-abiding citizens. What Marzette and his allies were doing in the criminal realm was essentially taking a stand for independence. In the lives of legitimate people, the minorities, frustration was at its highest level. Police brutality (much at the hands of a unit called STRESS), unemployment, housing and other forms of oppression had worn the black community down as far as it could possibly go. There was a fight brewing here too. Urban renewal projects leveled areas where the minority population lived (Chester's childhood home on Hague was one such example). There was black militancy urging the more hostile revolutionary action. Some clergy, particularly the Reverend Albert Cleague, spoke of separatism. People were listening. Harassment and humiliation, in almost every corner of their daily lives, had instilled absolute distrust and defiance within the community. The reality for many blacks in Detroit was a bleak one at best.

The boiling point occurred on Sunday July 23, 1967. In the very early hours, police raided an after hours establishment on the corner of 12th and Clairmount. Unlicensed bars such as this one were commonly called "blind pigs" and often the only place for blacks to go. The 1960's were a time a blatant racial inequality; therefore many minorities were not welcome in a number of white establishments.

A party for two returning Vietnam veterans grew to over eighty patrons inside this particular bar. When police arrived, they shut down the festivities and hauled a number of people off to jail – their intention was to literally arrest all eighty-two attendees. A crowd then gathered in protest. Two men, displaced and angry, kick started the looting. By the following day, an understaffed police presence could not handle what they initially thought would be a short-lived, contained riot. State Police were called in. The news media, at first, did not venture into the situation for fears of enabling "copy cat" uprisings, but soon the city realized this situation was far greater than anything they'd ever seen.

Over 200 fires were started and police arrested hundreds of looters. Many were taken to improvised jails and gave authorities fake names, making processing even more arduous for police. Eventually the National Guard was called in. Under the Insurrection Act of 1807, President Lydon Johnson was able to then send in army troops. Every major media force in the region then covered the events, as did many national outlets. This was momentous event, terrifying and confusing, yet was bound to occur sooner or later.

The violence continued until Thursday when relative order was restored. The damage, arrest, theft and death toll was incredibly high though. Some 1800 weapons had been stolen, both black and white owned establishments burned to the ground and forty-three people died. The riot also inspired uprisings in neighboring Michigan cities, though not to the extent of the 12th Street Riot.

Civil unrest had not disappeared while Chester Wheeler Campbell served his sentence in Jackson Prison. He was going to exit the facility and step back into a racially charged, tormented and shifting world.

What was occurring on the streets of Detroit was also happening in the drug world of Detroit. Minority drug dealers – large-scale dealers – were still under the control of the Italian Mafia. Not everyone in the black segment of the drug trade was particularly happy with this long-standing, otherwise accepted agreement.

Henry Marzette was so well established by the end of the 1960's that he could initiate the separatist movement. He already worked both sides of the law, so he knew the ins and outs of pay-offs and self-insulation from scrutiny. He was well versed in the methods and mindset of the Italian organized crime faction, having worked for them while in prison and later in the large-scale heroin invasion. He also knew how to get the product – without mafia traffickers' involvement. Marzette was ready to offer black drug lords the option for true power and liberation from what he considered an oppressive situation – the mob's ruling power. The hour of reprisal was almost here.

CHAPTER EIGHT

DIALOGUE OF A HIT MAN

"Don't lie, tell one lie, then you gotta tell another lie to compound on the first."
– Meyer Lansky

For the murder of Luther Mixon, which occurred during a botched robbery attempt at a known gambling den in 1955, Chester Wheeler Campbell had served over thirteen years in the Jackson Prison. While in prison, Campbell's familiar stomping ground of West Detroit was being reshaped, at least in the criminal elements, by the former cop turned drug lord Henry Marzette. The kingpin was restructuring the criminal socio-economic landscape of the Motor City into one that favored the independence black dealers from the longstanding Italian rulers; Chester was anxious to return to this place. He was about to catch a break. Campbell had filed motions for a retrial and was finally granted one in the fall of 1969. This time around, Campbell was going to plea bargain, hoping to be set free on 'time served' if he played his cards right. In order to do so though, Campbell would have to actually explain the circumstances of the crime – something the career criminal had not previously done. He was very reserved; a silent tongue. Nevertheless, here was a chance to achieve some legal relief, and he would comply – but not without a few reservations.

On September 12th Chester Wheeler Campbell and his attorney S. Allen Early entered the Recorder's Court in Detroit, and stood before Judge Robert L. Evans. Representing 'The People' was Assistant Prosecutor Terrance Boyle. No jury. Chester wanted a quick and to the point result; he was in court to plead guilty to murder in the second degree.

Judge Evans went through the necessary legal motions, explaining to Campbell the option to have a trial by jury, and making sure the defendant was not coerced into his decision to waive that and other options. Chester politely gave the 'yes' and 'no' answers to the series of standard questions. Judge Evans was satisfied, so he moved on to questioning Campbell about the original charges. Specific questions relating to the 1955 murder he was originally convicted of.

Judge Evans: *Mr. Campbell, on the first of July 1955, were you in the City of Detroit and involved in some sort of homicide?*
Campbell: *Yes, sir. I was.*
Judge Evans: *Do you know the name of the person that was killed?*
Campbell: *I think it was Luther Mixon.*
Judge Evans: *Do you know where he was killed?*
Campbell: *On the street.*
Judge Evans: *What Street?*
Campbell: *Lawton*
Judge Evans: *Do you know approximately what time?*
Campbell: *About 5:00 o'clock, I think.*
Judge Evans: *Tell me the circumstances of that incident.*

Campbell: *Prior to going to this Lawton address, I and several other fellows planned a robbery. After we got there and carried it out and in the process, my – I shot Mr. Mixon.*

Judge Evans: *You shot who?*

Campbell: *Luther Mixon.*

Judge Evans: *What do you mean you were carrying it out?*

Campbell: *What happened, well it's hard for me to reconstruct. I think that Mixon offered some resistance.*

Early: (Interjects) *He offered resistance to the robbery, is that it?*

Campbell: *Yes.*

Judge Evans: *What do you mean offered resistance?*

Campbell: *I think he made an attempt to approach me in some way.*

Judge Evans: *What do you mean he approached you?*

Campbell: *He started toward me.*

Judge Evans: *What were you doing when he started toward you?*

Campbell: *I had a gun.*

Judge Evans: *Did Mr. Mixon have the money you were after?*

Campbell: *We assumed he did.*

Judge Evans: *You assumed he did.*

Campbell: *We assumed he did.*

Judge Evans: *Had you said anything to Mr. Mixon before he began to approach you?*

Campbell: *In what respect?*

Judge Evans: *Anything, had you said anything to him?*

Campbell: *We indicated it was a stick-up.*

Judge Evans: *You indicated that?*

Campbell: *Yes.*

Judge Evans: *Do you recall what if anything Mr. Mixon said?*

Campbell: *I don't know, I don't believe he said anything.*

Judge Evans: *Your recollection is he said nothing up until the time he began to approach you, is that right?*

Campbell: *Something was said about a car, but I don't recall exactly what was said.*

Judge Evans: *In any event he began to approach you and then what happened?*

Campbell: *I hit him with the pistol.*

Judge Evans: *You hit him with what part of the - you hit him with part of the pistol?*

Campbell: *Yes.*

Judge Evans: *By that you mean you didn't shoot him, you struck him with the pistol itself?*

Campbell: *Yes.*

Judge Evans: *Then what happened?*

Campbell: *It went off.*

Judge Evans: *It went off... was Mr. Mixon shot when the pistol went off?*

Campbell: *It was the only shot that was fired. That's the only one.*

Judge Evans: *What happened after Mr. Mixon was on the ground, where did the bullet strike him?*

Campbell: *Somewhere in the head.*

Judge Evans: *After that what happened?*

Campbell: *I think I went through his pockets.*

Judge Evans: *Did you take anything from his pockets?*

Campbell: *Took some money.*

Judge Evans: *Now you said before that time... did I understand you to say before this happened you had planned to rob, had you planned to rob Mr. Mixon?*

Campbell: *Not him in particular no. The place was supposed to have been a numbers house.*

Judge Evans: *Did you know Mr. Mixon was going to be there?*

Campbell: *No.*

Judge Evans: *Did you have any reason to suspect he was going to be there?*

Campbell: *We knew certain people would be there who were involved in numbers.*

Judge Evans: *You had planned to rob anyone that happened to be there regardless of who it was?*

Campbell: *Yes sir, it was the house itself, regardless of who was there we assumed the place was a numbers place.*

Judge Evans: *Now when you say we, how many do you mean?*

Campbell: *The fellows I was working with.*

Judge Evans: *Who was with you?*

Campbell: *Do I have to say that?*

Judge Evans: *If you offer a plea, yes.*

Early: (interjects) *You are not copping out when you say who it was.*

Campbell: *Watson Brooks.*

Judge Early: *Who Else?*

Campbell: *David Green.*

Judge Early: *Did they have pistols also?*

Campbell: *One did.*

Following the testimony given, Judge Evans asked Campbell if he was sure he wanted a sentence immediately delivered. Campbell did indeed, and his attorney reiterated to the court how his client had already served thirteen years prison time in Southern Michigan. The judge asked the prosecutor if he had any objections, which he did not.

"Mr. Campbell," Judge Evans commenced, "it is the sentence of this court that you be committed to the custody of the Corrections Commission for a minimum period of thirteen years and maximum of twenty years. You have credit for the time you have already spent in Jackson."

With that delivery, and apart from some expected formalities through the interim, Chester Wheeler Campbell was on well his way to freedom, but far from entertaining the concept of a legitimate existence. He was going to return to the *wild, wild West Detroit* – an area now endemic with components of brewing chaos, charged and volatile factions within the underworld at the doorstep of war with each other. This was just the sort of environment Chester Wheeler Campbell was prepared for and anxious to be a part of. It was a place where Henry Marzette and other aspiring and established black drug kingpins were at odds with each other, the police and the mafia. Chester would fit in superbly.

Upon his release, Campbell hit the ground running, eagerly staking his claim in the narcotics underworld drama. He stepped back into society ready to buy some new suits, a few untraceable weapons, and of course reconnect with some old pals and make a few new ones. Chester Wheeler Campbell entertained the career options of an enforcer role. He also entertained the ladies, criminal associates and other unsavory characters. A little celebration was had before work began, but Chester was first and foremost interested in business.

For the first few years of his freedom, Campbell tried to lie relatively low, but not entirely out of law enforcement's vision. He was definitely up to no good. Wayne County lawmen were aware of him, beginning to learn the extent of which Chester was developing his reputation for high-priced and elaborate murder plots. In the wake of his free reign – from 1969 to 1975 – Campbell's name was being loosely connected to at least ten drug-related murders. His business was raided by narcotics officers, which they found heroin, and, he was arrested in connection with the murder of a man named Bernard Mooten. He reentered the Motor City at the dawn of a two-year dope war, and was deeply involved in the battles. The real horrors of what Chester was thought to be doing started to unfold in Orchard Lake after his unceremonious arrest, but it was during the war that he honed those skills. Amazingly, he was catching some breaks with the drug busts. His lawyers were keeping him out of jail, but again, he was definitely chalking up warrants and drawing the attention of Detroit's organized crime investigators.

CHAPTER NINE

DOPE WARS

*He that is of the opinion money will do everything may well be
suspected of doing everything for money.*
– Benjamin Franklin

NINETEEN-SIXTY-NINE rolled in and Chester Wheeler Campbell rejoiced in his freedom. On September 18, he was officially a free man, ready to take on a criminal position that many were trying but few had the innate capacity to fulfill. A genuine enforcer, not just a thug – Campbell would never, in his own mind at least, reduce himself to low level bullying. He wanted to raise the standards. Many underworld figures in Detroit viewed him as just that sort of guy, one who could indeed carry out a job and keep his mouth closed. He would have ample opportunities to prove his mettle as the seventies rolled in.

Crime legend points directly to Henry Marzette as the single most influential and dividing organized crime figure in the great shift and power struggle of drug dealers. His rise to power transpired while Chester Campbell was housed in Jackson Prison. Much had gone on in the Motor City since Chester's time away from the streets, but he would find plenty of business opportunities in the environment created by increased drug addiction, corruption and the impending dope war that Henry Marzette's ideals were ushering in.

Marzette was the ringleader behind a large meeting of black drug lords– arranged to discuss the aforementioned 'exodus' from mob reliance, dubbed "Little Apalachin of Detroit" in the summer of 1971(an obvious reference to the infamous mafia meeting fiasco of 1957 in Apalachin, New York). The former cop had been considering, quite seriously, doing business independent of the mafia for years. He had already taken the steps to bypass the mob's stranglehold on importation of the drug. He felt the blacks had basically been doing most of the work on the streets anyway; so taking it to the next level was only natural – and necessary. His meeting was called to address, in the presence of every major black dealer from all sides of Greater Detroit, the separatist movement and how it could be achieved with success. Further issues on the table included how to define all the territories of dealing and who would control them. By the time "Little Apalachin" was held, Marzette's fondness for independence and setting himself up for maintaining a top position throughout the drug hierarchy had culminated in war. The infamous meeting itself did not start the fireworks; the rumblings were already taking shape in the form of rival hits and raids. It did however drive the final nail into a proverbial coffin for many drug pushers, ushering in a phase that – long term – would forever change the scope of narcotics dealing. Whites would, one day, have very little control over the heroin and cocaine business.

The details of Little Apalachin trickled out through street rumors and police informants. The event was not met with universal appeal, contrary to what Marzette may have hoped. As crime historian Scott Burnstein puts it, "He called on all the major dealers to organize against the Italians. There was a group of people that did and a group that didn't. Between 70 and 72 and that was the first ripples of or the sign of the future – blacks developing independence. That's why you had unrest in the 70's that didn't exist before that."

The major mafia drug brokers at the time were "Papa John" Priziola, Jimmy Quasarano and Peter Vitale. They were the top end guys responsible for managing importation of narcotics. The "street level" mobsters that oversaw the dope distribution to the black faction included a pair of siblings well known in the Detroit underworld.

"Lower tier, in terms of drugs on wholesale drug dealings, were done by the Giacalone brothers. They had the guys moving the drugs Quasarano was bringing in.

Mostly heroin," Burnstein explains.

The Italian Mafia had exclusively controlled most of the heroin entering Detroit since they took power of organized crime after prohibition ended. Marzette probably didn't care much of who was doing it; just that he wanted none of the mob's people involved in his business anymore.

Some black dealers were, and wished to remain, loyal to the mob controlled heroin business. The resistance may have taken Marzette aback. This idea of independence was to an otherwise logical and practical suggestion. He was offering all these dealers (mostly West Detroiters) not only the opportunity to be independent, but also how to do so. Nevertheless, there were a number of them that agreed and a number who did not.

"Those that didn't," Burnstein adds, "went to the Italians and about a two year war broke out."

The war was not just about loyalty either. Marzette's ruling power even prior to the 1971 meeting had been a subject of controversy within the drug dealing community. Not everyone wanted to do things his way; some thought they could achieve independence all by themselves – freedom from Henry Marzette included.

Although historically it was a very rare occurrence for anyone "in the know" to speak to police, a few did – anonymously- and of course the grapevine reaches all segments of society. Cops knew the meeting had taken place and they were very aware of the potential fallout. The most immediate, prominent example of such consequence involved another prominent dealer who was in attendance at Marzette's grand meeting. Nual Steele wasn't impressed with the lines Marzette had drawn for territory and trafficking sources. Word travelled quickly around town that the twenty-six year old high roller Steele told Marzette what he really thought of the whole plan and stormed out in a defiant manner. Steel had no interest in Marzette's edicts, particularly the boundaries and territory issues. This move did not sit well with West Detroit's most powerful drug lord. A message would have to be sent - so any and all other potential challengers would swiftly be reminded of what happens to dissidents.

These major breaking points for the city's upper and under-world were not to be scoffed at. Chester Wheeler Campbell surely knew what social and economic status of Detroit had become since his time away in prison. Now he was about to stake his own claim in an era of despair. He often viewed the world as oppressive, albeit selfishly, but still a further justification for his outlaw behavior.

In West Detroit, death and dope dealing were already commonplace by 1970. While many perceived Henry Marzette as the chief drug lord, there were plenty of underlings and other aspiring dealers who were staging their own forms of territory takeovers. Some were working with Marzette; some on their own. One of the dealers making a name in the region was Milton "Happy" Battle. Battle was no small time hood. He was interested in cocaine and heroin, and made a lot of money from the sale of both. His home was furnished with a cedar chest – filled to capacity with cash. He had acquired police contacts and protection; money laundering associates. His close friend and associate, George Dudley, was a thoroughly violent type who enjoyed lining enemies up against a select wall, in his own house, and filling them with bullets. They often used a thirty-year old addict named Wiley Reed for jobs, courier and enforcer his primary roles. Reed would be a very pivotal figure – a huge threat against the day-to-day operations and payoffs – in the coming years.

Conversely, a small time gangster named Robert Lee Gardner was also working the Detroit expanse, trying to establish his own distribution and sales territory. Gardner, however, was also a thief and known for selling tainted or "bad" dope. Other dealers were concerned not only with his frequent stick-ups of rival dope houses, but also his distribution of garbage heroin. Some of the upper level dealers were considered more scrupulous, not wanting their customer base to die off from bad product. Gardner was making enemies quickly by muscling in on reputable trade regions and the sale of poor product to the regular customers of other, more established dealers.

As for the dozen top drug lords on the other side of the city – police called them *The East Detroit Twelve*. Though powerful in their own right, none of the drug lords in the East did had garnered as much notoriety as Henry Marzette was in the

West. Police still felt he was the fattest cat of all the Motor City's kingpins.

Both East and West Detroit was feeling the effects of gang warfare. Dealers of every level were being robbed and executed by rivals; the addicts were being killed too, like collateral damage. Marzette was being challenged; yet still the ruling power in West Detroit. Chester Wheeler Campbell was gaining quite a reputation for his enforcement ability in the West, not to mention making some important business contacts in the East as well.

Despite the lack of press reportage on Marzette's exploits, locals from these streets and law enforcement entities were very aware. From approximately 1970 to 1972 the struggle raged between Marzette's loyalists who sought independence and the kingpins that chose to remain in good standing with the mob, or attempted to go solo. Police, however, seemed to be turning a blind eye to their former brethren, the direct link to underworld warfare he kick started, and his newfound financial gain.

Henry Marzette was visibly the boss, and so he wanted to remain. He travelled around town in luxury cars, wore the finest suits and people knew he was the top dog. Marzette's determination to give black drug dealers independence from mafia control was met with a split decision during his "Little Apalachin" meeting in 1970. The divide was not a mere "agree to disagree" scenario. That doesn't happen in the drug trade. The situation was dynamic; rival black dealers, mafia factions, paid police protectors, all made for a rapidly spiraling bad situation much worse for the city.

Money brings out the worst in people sometimes, so too for drug dealers. Blood was spilling throughout Detroit. Marzette's allies and his detractors all played a deadly game of assassination, intimidation, payoffs and rip-offs. Marzette's meeting was held in July; Nual Steel was the first major enemy to be made an example of just one month later. While inside a nightclub in West Detroit (one of several frequented by underworld clientele), Nual Steel and his bodyguard fell victim to a hail of gunfire, courtesy of unknown assassins rumored to have been sent by Marzette.

The war raged on. Another dealer on the West Side who openly argued for nonalignment was Willie Flowers. He was gunned down in March for not only desiring independence in his drug business, but also for attempting to set up sovereign gambling and prostitution operations. This move could've earned him a death sentence from any number of sources: rival drug dealers or the mob (gambling and prostitution were predominantly overseen by mafia factions).

Detroit's murder toll had reached beyond the three hundred mark by June of 1971. Police Inspector James Bannon addressed the post-*Little Apalachin* violence, saying barely more than, "Things did heat up." Conservative estimates considered at least forty or fifty those deaths as people with direct or past associations in the drug business, slaughtered in the war that kicked off shortly following Henry Marzette's "Little Apalachin" in the summer of 1970.

The most brutal of incidents happened just before dawn on June 14, 1971. Robert Lee Gardner answered a knock on his door only to be greeted by four gun-wielding intruders. They fired three rounds into his body and left him for dead. The group of killers then ransacked first floor apartment of Gardner's two-story brick house, located just a half block from where the 1967 riots began. The foursome fired their weapons at anyone and everyone they could find in the place. It was a bloodbath. Seven people shot dead on the spot in Gardner's home, four jumped out windows and escaped into the alleyways. The media reported that one of the escapees called the police; other sources stated that Gardner's wife called the authorities after she returned to home at around 4:30 a.m.

When police arrived at around 4:30 a.m., they found the bodies of four women and three men. All were young and black, late teens to early twenties. Three of the female victims had been bound with a cord, around the wrists in front of their bodies; the men were not bound at all. All seven were killed in a deliberate fashion, shot in the head at close range. All of the dead were found scattered within the living room area of the home. 10th Precinct investigator, Lieutenant Charles Boutin, commented of the scene, "It appears to be an execution type, perhaps related to drugs." To everyone else, the drug element was obvious. There was plenty of heroin residue found throughout the home, syringes, plus a half-dozen weapons, including shotguns and handguns. The police, however, were largely reticent about ever calling the events of the last year or so as a "dope war." It wasn't that they were collectively in denial, but officially it was not referred to in such terms. Because the crime was so heinous, the media was all over the scene, but of course police had the entire house secured. By daylight though, neighbors began coming for a look and some were willing to talk to press. The police hadn't released any of the deceased names, but a curious pair of youths approached a reporter and asked how many were killed. The reporter told them seven and one of the pair said a victim was his brother. The other youth simply said, "Benny, Gale and Willy," in reference to other victims. Another onlooker told reporters that nobody really knew the people that lived in the house, only that the blinds were always down and young people frequented the place. The brutality and despair caused by the drug trade alone was wearing an already tired community down further. Another

neighbor told reporters just what it's like to live like this, saying
-"With the way crime is around here you have nothing to do
with people you know nothing about, especially with so much
drugs around here."

The effect of the so-called dope war was undeniable. This time
it wasn't a dealer on dealer hit. Most of those murdered in Gardner's house, and the handful that got away, were all users, addicts.
Gardner dealt to customers and provided them with a place to
consume the product. "We are not saying they were selling dope
there," commented District Inspector James Bannon. "Maybe
they were, but at the moment all we can do is to report what we
found here." Regardless of hesitance, on the part of authorities,
to call the situation 'drug-related' – Gardner's house was a dope
den, and his enemies did not care about collateral damage. Gardner was obviously the prime target for the assassins, but the war
had escalated to a point where anyone was fair game. Plus, there
could never be witnesses. The press dubbed the incident "The
Detroit Massacre." Just days later, Gardner's associate, a dealer
named Gerald Williams, was found shot to death.

Robert Lee Gardner, mortally wounded during the attack on
his dope den, lingered in critical condition at Ford Hospital for
another week before the reaper took him. He never spoke of who
the perpetrators were.

Rumors circulated that both Gardner and Williams "had a
contract put out on them." Anonymous sources spoke of the hit
being issued by East Side dealers… in retaliation for the duo's
hawking of bad and fake heroin – to other dealers – and the
frequent robberies of East Side dope dens. Although some arguments were made that the more established drug lords were
honorable in the sense of "concern" for their customer's, exactly
how genuinely "scrupulous" the old school legion of dealers was

caused skepticism. The murders around town were still ultimately about who controlled what, including customers. Of course they did not want their customers to get bad dope and die off, but how "ethical" dealers were, well, they were undeniably providing a poison – high grade or not, still a drug that was ruining many lives.

Even with a deadly two-year blood lust from all dealers on all fronts in Detroit, Henry Marzette's uncanny knack for running so powerfully under the radar wasn't' brought into public question until, when, in 1972, John Nichols – a police commissioner – was called to answer allegations in front of city council. The council wanted to know if he or any other law enforcement officer actually protected the kingpin.

Within the slight amounts of press coverage that existed, a series of articles written by a Detroit Free Press writer named Howard Kohn addressed the subject of bribery, thereby lighting the council's fire on this subject (This was the same Howard Kohn that Chester Wheeler Campbell kept news clippings of several years later). In his commentary, Kohn pointed to quotes from anonymous police officers admitting that Marzette could never have pulled off a $5 million a year operation without paying bribes to cops. This was a scathing allegation, but a very probable scenario in a business that requires many 'payoffs' to survive.

Marzette, however, could not be questioned directly by the council, or anybody else for that matter. By the time this inquiry began, it was too late - he had passed away just days earlier. The former cop turned kingpin died, according to the press, "while he slept in his modest Highland Park home," in 1972 of kidney failure at the age of 45.

Adding to the enigma of Henry Marzette's life and death was a 1973 editorial piece titled *"Minorities Rising Fast in Narcotics Heirarchy"* that ran in the Los Angeles Times. The article delved even further into the questionable story of Marzette's demise. Times staff writer Francis Ward wrote, "Marzette reportedly died in Detroit last year, but his death has never been clearly established."

Conspiracy theories aside and assuming the drug lord did in fact pass away; Marzette remained as lavish in death as he was in life. His funeral service was an over-the-top spectacle for those attending, which included friends, associates, and the police. The police were suspicious though. For someone who died of kidney failure – not any outwardly disfiguring circumstance – an open casket for people to give last respects would be expected. Not the case for Henry Marzette. His was a closed casket affair. Reporter Ward referenced law enforcement recollections of the guarded event, adding, "At his 'funeral,' Marzette's toughs refused to open his casket, the police sources said, and there has never been an official death certificate issued for him."

Just as in life, Henry Marzette's death left authorities with questions that could not, or would not be answered by anyone who was privy to the inner world of the kingpin. Regardless of what really did or did not happen to Henry Marzette in 1972, one development was for certain – there would be someone to fill the void.

CHAPTER TEN

DIARY OF A HIT MAN

"The desire of knowledge, like the thirst for riches, increases ever with the acquisition of it."
-**Laurence Sterne**

WHAT IS MORE powerful than the intimidating collection of weapons Chester Campbell amassed? More fearsome than the steely-eyed look he gave? Of far more value than his expensive wardrobe or jewelry and property? Knowledge, that's what. Nothing, not even an arsenal of guns or an unscrupulous attitude can produce the sort of fear in people that *information* can. From the dawn of time to modern day – knowledge makes oppressive governments paranoid, puts religious groups on edge, and assures corporations get jittery when business practices are called into question. All it takes is one pervasive individual to gather, contemplate and exercise greater senses of intelligence based on knowledge to either change something for the better, or for worse. Either way, the power of 'knowing' is worth more than gold. Acquiring intelligence, in more ways than one, was exactly how Chester Wheeler Campbell maintained an aura of power. His business was not corporate, religious, or governmental. Campbell's was a direct result of, a necessity within the business of heroin.

Chester Wheeler Campbell knew things. He had collected information so valuable, and potentially damning, that anyone and everyone from both sides of the law became fearful. That is the power of knowledge, and Campbell kept meticulous records of information, handwritten, fully exploited in notebooks. For Detroit's organized criminals, the narcotics trade in particular; Chester Wheeler Campbell was indeed the most dangerous enforcer because he was armed with data, descriptions, and diagrams. He had been gathering data on everyone and anyone remotely involved in the underworld of Detroit and beyond. Years of intelligence gathering, really from the moment he exited the gate of Jackson Prison, Chester was not one to sit idle. His criminal acumen was second to none by the early 1970's. Chester Wheeler Campbell scribbled, scrawled, drew, typed, and visually or audibly recorded every bit of information he could acquire on enemies and allies alike. It was like a diary of sorts.

The Motor City Hit Man didn't keep a diary of his everyday thoughts and feelings; he kept a journal of everything going on in the drug underworld of Detroit Michigan. His diary was not a memoir, but rather a collection of lists, addresses, properties, license plate numbers and phone numbers. Campbell's notebooks were a reflection of just how corrupt, sinister and realistic the drug trade in Detroit's underworld was.

The notes contained locations of witnesses, dealers, safe houses, and details for homes of law enforcement officials. Campbell kept track of unsolved murder and drug cases; he had access to cops on the kingpins' payrolls. This is the sort of information that truly strikes fear into people. He gathered information in every conceivable manner. Surveillance, gossip, shadowing, payoffs, and keeping in the know by simply 'talking' to contacts, Campbell did it all. These were all easily applied methods of assembling intelligence. From mobsters to motorcycle clubs, hookers to hit men, pushers to pimps, Chester Wheeler Campbell made the rounds from Detroit to Cleveland, keeping tabs on everyone even remotely involved in underworld business. Everything was jotted down within the pages of his notebook collection.

When Orchard Lake police officers John Walsh and Edward Beyett removed the notebooks from Campbell's rented Oldsmobile trunk – the true story began to emerge. Again, the police had no idea just how important the paperwork in Chester Wheeler Campbell's possession really was at first glance. Over the coming weeks though, officials in neighboring Wayne County would jump on board the investigation and give insight they were already privy to on the Detroit strongarm.

One of the first items to draw law enforcement's ire… a list of presumed future 'hit' targets, which included a well-known Assistant Prosecutor in Oakland County named L. Brooks Patterson. The initial review of Campbell's notes led to the assumption that at least 300 names of individuals were recorded; presumably all potential targets of the assassin, yet in reality many were simply associates and contacts. Contrary to the often overly hyped press coverage at the time, Patterson's name, as were many of the others, not explicitly noted in Campbell's book as *targets*. In some cases, Patterson's being one such example; names were simply scrawled on a page. Nevertheless, there were enough signs pointing to the danger of anyone having their name in any of Chester's books. So, upon receiving the disturbing news that he was blatantly referenced in Campbell's notes – Patterson was given around the clock extra security. This was unprecedented before

Chester Campbell entered the picture. The standard way of law and order in both Oakland and Wayne counties was changing abruptly, thanks to the revelations gleaned from Chester's collection of written materials.

Investigators were also very interested in what appeared to be a list of at least ten names recognized as belonging to unsolved-murder victim cases. All of the murders were considered drug-related, and Campbell was immediately presumed, in the minds of many who read and deciphered his notebooks, as somehow 'involved' in each case. There was no proof as such that Campbell had killed anyone on the list, of course, but the information was enough for cops to consider looking much deeper into each unexplained case.

Campbell had made notations of addresses where witnesses were being kept. He sometimes neatly – often times sloppily - wrote detailed, semi-detailed and a lot of 'coded' information, down to the license plates, of lawmen and dope peddlers alike. Many streets in and around the Pingree area were listed; safe houses, drug dens and protected witnesses. Nobody was off limits for the hit man. Everyone who heard the news or had been involved in examining the notebooks was, quite understandably, uneasy with the revelations of one Chester Wheeler Campbell. Though the man himself spoke very little to authorities, his possessions were loud proclamations of his dangerous presence in the Motor City and beyond.

Though the press sometimes alluded to Campbell possessing one, or a handful of notebooks – the fact was Chester Wheeler Campbell kept dozens of notebooks. They varied in size and content, many purchased for the bargain price of nineteen cents a piece. Within many of the pages were questions he'd asked himself. He used the pages in some for the purpose of accounting;

payoffs, drug transactions and debts especially. He even maintained records of his own arrests... and associates who were implicated with him. Campbell also used some of the notebooks for record keeping in his 'legitimate' – legal assistant - work he performed for attorney Wilfrid Rice.

Most unusual and disconcerting to authorities, however, was the realization that Campbell also had access to Michigan's *Law Enforcement Information Network* system – LEIN. Yes, a hit man in Detroit's underworld had the ability to access the official mechanism for "information sharing" – exclusive to the criminal justice system since its inception in 1967. This was both illegal and unprecedented. How did Chester Wheeler Campbell obtain LEIN records? The answer lay in a very sketchy, gray area that spanned across the lines of crime, law and politics. Somehow Campbell, or his drug lord employers, had 'insiders' working on their behalf. What he was using the LEIN for specifically – to identify the owners of every vehicle license plate he recorded.

CHAPTER ELEVEN

DENIAL OF
A HIT MAN

*"Watch your thoughts; they become words. Watch your words; they be-
come actions. Watch your actions; they become habits. Watch your habits;
they become character. Watch your character; it becomes your destiny."*
- Unknown

JUST A WEEK after Chester was arrested in Orchard
Lake, his ostentatious team of attorneys went before
Judge Robert B. Webster in Pontiac Michigan. It was
Tuesday the 14th, a day that established Campbell's familiarity
and perhaps his camaraderie with one of his lawyers and possibly even some members of law enforcement. The purpose of the
court appearance was for Campbell's defense to basically paint
a better picture of him. His bond was set at $400,000 by this
point. The plan was to have one of his own counsels – Wilfrid C.
Rice - take the witness stand, while the other – Elbert Hatchett
and prosecutor – Richard Thompson – cross-examined him. The
defense wanted to lower the bond and get their client out of jail.

Rice was sworn in and took the stand. Thompson asked the
Judge for one restriction; the defense is limited to just one witness. Hatchett agreed, stating only Rice would testify. The Judge

was satisfied and questioning began by Hatchett. The expected series of questions were presented to Rice, i.e. profession, address and relationship to the defendant.

Hatchett asked Rice how long he's known Chester and how often they encounter each other. "I have represented Mr. Campbell in various and sundry matters since 1970 both civil and criminal matters," Rice explained. "In the last two years I would say I have seen him an average of four to five days per week." Rice openly admitted he had both a professional and social relationship with Campbell, stating they two met often at the law office, but also in Rice's home and at a business establishment – a clothing store – he owned on Woodward Avenue in Detroit. The witness also told the court of times when Campbell would chat with police officers he encountered in public places, such as restaurants. What may at first seem like a damning conflict of interest was actually a ploy to portray Chester as a decent guy who was by no means hiding from the law. Rice's admission of a friendly relationship with Campbell was also aimed at disproving the prosecution's notion of him being an evil character out to kill.

What transpired thereafter was intended to further paint a picture of Chester as smart, charismatic, likeable and even afraid for his own life. But the defense was careful how they addressed the issue of Campbell's reputation as a "hit man" – a subject that was certainly going to be brought up again during the proceedings.

First, Rice was asked his awareness of Chester's past criminal record, of which he said he was only knowledgeable regarding incidents from 1956 on. Then, the subject of Campbell's taxes was initiated. Rice told the court he knew Campbell filed taxes from 1970 through 1972, and had even qualified for hefty returns (over two-thousand dollars in 1972). The tax questions segued into what, exactly, Chester Wheeler Campbell did for a living.

Hatchett: *Now, what is his occupation, if you know?*

Rice: *Mr. Campbell has several businesses. He is the owner and operator of Wheelers Total Service at 8505 Oakland Avenue in Detroit Michigan. He has an interest in the Club 4800 at Warren and McGraw and he has interest in a funeral home in Detroit.*

Rice also mentioned Campbell having invested money with other individuals pertaining to entertainment venues; a roller rink and social hall among them. The club Chester owned or managed – 4800 - was better known as *Skeeter's*, and affectionately named after one of his many lady friends. In any event, based on the information spoken to that point, Hatchett opened the door for questioning on Chester's skills and talents. Rice essentially spoke of Campbell as a legal prodigy.

"In my opinion," Rice stated, "He is an expert in criminal law and an expert in writing legal briefs. He had done research for me and other lawyers that I can name and he has done investigations for me and interviewed people for me in the Wayne County Jail and Jackson State Prison. I can indicate that I have been very successful with the brief that he has written in which I have engaged his services."

And then the query of Campbell's alleged "other" profession was addressed. Hatchett asked Rice if he was familiar with the "hit man" label and what that term denoted. Rice responded affirmatively, but did not believe Campbell showed him any reason to suggest he was indeed an assassin.

"I am more inclined to believe he was a fearful person," Rice explained. "I think that is manifested in the fact, that when he was arrested, he had a cocked weapon in his possession."

The critical term Rice used, *fearful*, was suggesting that Campbell was merely a man who had enemies or was, for whatever reason, concerned for his own safety, particularly when doing jobs for Rice. The defense was portraying him on the contrary to his reputation as inducing fear in others. Rice asserted Chester was anything but a "cold blooded killer."

Rice was also asked about the documents Campbell had in his possession, specifically the notebooks with names of private citizens and law enforcement officials, and a copy of Grand Jury transcripts.

Hatchett: *Now, Mr. Rice you are aware of the fact that from his personal belonging were taken by the prosecutor's office and that was a transcript involving the Wayne County Grand Jury proceedings, is that correct?*

Rice: *Yes.*

Hatchett: *And in addition to that there were certain items and documents which purport to name public figures?*

Rice: *Yes.*

Hatchett: *What explanation can you offer in terms of the knowledge of Chester Wheeler Campbell for those items being in his possession?*

Rice: *Well, you Honor, all I can say is that from my experience with Mr. Campbell, I found that he is a person who has a habit of taking notes. In fact he always carries a notebook in his pocket and things that are of interest to him he jots down in the notebook and that's all the explanation I can give.*

Hatchett: *Isn't it a fact that Mr. Campbell did in fact have some contact with the Grand Jury proceedings in terms of what he had in his possession?*

Rice: *Yes, he was helping on an appeal and also worked on the appealing of the case of The People versus Willie B. Foster, who was one of the people indicted in that matter.*

Hatchett closed the questioning by asking Rice if Campbell

was actually avoiding police because of the alleged conspiracy charges against him. Wilfrid Rice maintained that Chester was friendly with cops, at least on one occasion as they were leaving the Peking Restaurant. Also, that the reason for Campbell's access to LEIN system was because he had been stopped for a traffic violation just a few months before his arrest in Orchard Lake.

Under cross-examination, Thompson questioned Rice on Campbell's criminal history from 1972. Thompson brought up an incident where Detroit police, specifically the 10th Precinct, searched Campbell's auto repair shop – Wheeler's Total Service – and confiscated a pound of drugs, which he referred to as cocaine. Rice kept his composure, simply correcting Thompson on the type of narcotics found, stating it was heroin. The prosecution also asked Rice questions about Chester's proprietary holdings and employment, more specific questions than Hatchett had asked. Rice explained that he assumed Campbell was not just an employee of Club 4800 because he took appointments, in his own office, within the establishment for situations that required "privacy." The skating rink, however, Rice though was just a place that Chester had rented out, as anyone could do. Thompson also wanted to know about the funeral home. Rice then told the court that Mary Williams was indeed Chester's girlfriend and that Campbell had remodeled the funeral home that she and her partner Evelyn Mason operated.

Thompson started digging for Rice's explanation on Campbell's notebook contents. Rice was obviously beginning to get irritated with the line of questioning. He asked Rice if it was Campbell's job then to keep the names of execution style hits in his notebook. Rice was visibly annoyed, and fired back at Thompson with feisty reply.

"No. I might point out, you know, that one of the names on that list of ten people you are talking about was a man named James Mattas who was Chester's closest friend and several of those people in that so called *ten*, those murders have been solved. They have been resolved down in the tenth precinct who killed those people. It is amusing to think that Chester would be involved in a crime which was already solved."

It got to the point where Hatchett was so determined to lower Campbell's bond to $20,000, telling Judge Webster that other people have received lower bond, people who have had guns, killed with those guns and larger quantities of drugs in their possession. The Judge calmly responded to Hatchett's plea by saying he had no recollection of such actions in his court. Hatchett knew Thompson wasn't going to let the issue go. Campbell was hit with $100,000 for each count in the Oakland County arrest. Three for weapons, one for drugs.

Hatchett also continued to argue the "hit man" label and its use – which he blamed fully on Thompson. Judge Webster reiterated to Hatchett that the label was not used, "No one in this courtroom has characterized your client as a hit man on this record."

Judge Webster, Richard Thompson and Hatchett all went back and forth on the issues. Hatchett eventually told the judge his vexation stating, "I submit what it was, was the Prosecutor's arguments to the press and everybody else that this man was a hit man. That's why he is in jail."

Elbert Hatchett beseeched to Judge Webster to lower Campbell's bond, reversing what they argued and condemned Judge Alice Gilbert for having set at $400,000. "How can there not be an abuse?" Hatchett asked the Judge. "How can this man or any man make four hundred thousand dollar bond? You say look at the record and this is not an abuse? You know it is a bond that he cannot make. You might as well tell him that he is not entitled to any bond at all because that would be what you are saying."

He went so far as saying he would rather resign as Chester's attorney than have to continue dealing with his unjustly incarcerated client. To drive his point home Hatchett continued, "This man is entitled to counsel and, your Honor, I cannot go over there to the jail every day trying to help this man. People kill people and are on bond and only difference is in fact that they happen to be perhaps a different color."

Elbert Hatchett was very aware of the racial issue, as a black man himself, and that his client was arrested in a very white part of Michigan. He wanted to make the point that some accused criminals get leeway, while others don't, based on factors that include race.

Still, the end result was not in favor of Chester Wheeler Campbell. "This court at this time," Judge Webster concluded, "cannot hold that the District Court Judge (Gilbert) abused her discretion in setting bond on the matter." And so it was. Chester was not leaving jail. Elbert Hatchett and Wilfrid Rice had an enemy of their own now. The legal team would meet again with Richard Thompson in the coming months. Things were about to get ugly in court.

Judge Alice Gilbert maintains she hadn't even been one to truly levy the heaviest bond on Campbell. "I set a reasonable bond, I thought. Then they brought the additional charges and my colleague set a high bond on one of the charges, nowhere near my amount." That said, she also remembers being convinced Campbell was a very dangerous character. Though she did not call him a 'hit man' in court, she says, "absolutely," she was sure the label was an appropriate term to describe what his true career entailed.

CHAPTER TWELVE

LOVE AND A FUNERAL HOME

"Proceed in angst when death is a common fortune."
- Anonymous

In the closing week of February 1975 it was time for law enforcement to launch full-scale raid on Chester Wheeler Campbell's home in West Detroit. And because it didn't take agents long to figure out exactly where Chester was going the night of February 6, when he ran Officer Sage of Keego Harbor PD off the road, an almost simultaneous raid was planned for yet another dwelling. The alleged 'hit man' – as he was now officially being called – was on his way to Commerce Road, also in the Orchard Lake area of Oakland County, where the home of Mary Williams stood.

Two houses were in the sights of police, and they had warrants allowing the search and seizure of a multitude of items. Guns and drugs were the obvious subjects of the search, but also any photographs, papers and other vestiges of criminal activity. Armed with such warrants, cops headed to one property in a scenic area of Oakland County, the other in a rough part of the Motor City in Wayne County. February 26 was a day of very productive police work that shed much light on Chester Wheeler Campbell's profession, lifestyle, interests and social activities.

First, Judge Elvin Davenport of Detroit's Recorder's Court signed a search warrant allowing Wayne County Organized Crime Task Force to search the home on Ivanhoe for, "all books, records or documents, including photographs relating to homicides and illegal drug transactions and all guns and bullets." Detroit investigators raced to Chester's home on Ivanhoe with the intention of gathering a mother lode of evidence. Since Campbell had been incarcerated for several weeks now, and assuming nobody else had tampered with his house in the interim, cops expected a speedy entrance and search process.

The agents broke down the front door and quickly began probing inside the two-story brick and sided structure, plus the detached garage. They found some of the suspected and assorted photographs, paperwork, receipts, and books that were similar in nature to those discovered in his vehicle after the Orchard Lake arrest. These items were all permitted for confiscation per the issued search warrant.

Then the search revealed suspected narcotics, another cache of weapons and a large amount of cash. Removed from Campbell's were staggering amounts of money - approximately $280,100 (though Campbell later claimed cops took over $525,000 in cash). His weapon stash at the house was also stunning, a find of no less than three rifles and eleven more handguns. Police removed all the items, including the cash. Meanwhile Oakland County investigators were preparing their surprise visit to Commerce Road. Mary Williams wasn't believed to be any sort of potential 'target', as many names in the 'notebooks' were thought to be. She was not on any list, but rather Chester's principal romantic interest of the time, as his attorney Wilfrid Rice verified in Judge Webster's court. Remarkably – perhaps paradoxically – Campbell's lover happened to be a funeral director by trade – which investigators were also aware of. Or, maybe that was a perfect love connection after all: the hit man and the funeral director. Interestingly, one of the receipts found in Chester's possession included a membership fees statement for the Michigan Licensed Beverage Association – addressed to the club known as *Skeeter's*, with the attention to - Romeo and Mary C. Williams. Romeo was in fact Mary Williams deceased husband. Mary could have indeed been the one Chester called 'Skeeter.' Regardless, investigators were cognizant of Chester's relationship with Williams, as an employee, as an investor and as a lover. So, her place was a clear target of interest.

Police quickly discovered that along with co-owner Evelyn Mason, Chester's girlfriend operated the Mason-Williams Funeral Home in Detroit. The establishment formerly known as E.M. Mason Funeral Home sat on the corner of Oakland and Alger, not far from the portion of Hague Street where Campbell was raised.

Just following the raid on Campbell's Ivanhoe home, law enforcement officers from various divisions, along with the OLPD, were ready to pay Williams an official visit. First, Chief Prosecutor Richard Thompson called Officer Gordon Hays of Orchard Park, requesting he "stake out" the home located in the 4900 block of Commerce Road. The request was made just minutes after 6:00 p.m. on the evening of February 26. Joining Hays were fellow Orchard Lake officers Corporal Walsh and Edward Beyett.

The weather was relatively mild. No precipitation that day and temps lingered around 35 degrees into sundown. Tolerable for a winter stakeout, but as Officers sat patiently in their vehicles, waiting for Mary Williams to return home, evening hours waned and nightfall approached. The Wayne County investigators didn't have to wait when conducting the raid on Chester's home, as they weren't staking anyone out. For Oakland County officials though, an already slow night was about to grow even longer on Commerce Road.

Four hours after cops began the surveillance mission on Commerce Road... Mary Williams finally arrived. The waiting game, however, would continue.

Williams pulled into her driveway at 10:25 p.m. only to be startled by the slamming car doors and approaching police officers. Cops greeted her not with a search warrant, but with an advance notice the warrant was on its way.

Officer Hays explained that Chief Prosecutor Thompson would be arriving shortly with a warrant to search her home in regards to the belongings of Chester Wheeler Campbell. Yet, it was not until 11:00 p.m. that Judge Ingraham was visited at his home by Gary Hawkins, affiant of the warrant. The judge signed the papers and Hawkins was off and running.

The warrant arrived and was presented to Williams. Without incident, she let investigators in. Upon entering the basement area of the home, she was asked by Hawkins if Chester kept any belongings at this residence. "Yes," she said, pointing to a room in the center of the basement. "He keeps things here."

Things indeed. The team of investigators, which included officers from the Oakland County Task Force and Detroit Organized Crime Force, took note of a room with wood paneling and carpeted floors located in the central area of the basement. Within this room, Williams pointed out clothing and other personal affects that she said belonged to Campbell. The rate at which they were discovering suspect items, particularly drugs and unusually large amounts of cash, had become commonplace. Discovery of similar items, within this basement room at his girlfriend's house, was certainly no surprise. Besides Chester's clothing in a closet, they also noticed scrapbooks located in this little area of William's home. Not the typical book of family photos and heirlooms. These were different. Campbell liked to keep mementos: newspaper clippings of murder and drug bust stories, photographs and more. He was definitely following the bizarre events related to Detroit Free Press reporter Howard Kohn (the reporter had himself become the subject of controversy after claims he was kidnapped by people within the drug underworld, but was accused by others of manufacturing the story). Campbell's area has held more receipts, personal letters, correspondence to other known underworld figures, love letters, and a collection of erotic photographs –instant pictures from his land camera. From the photographs, it was apparent that Mary Williams was not his only object of sexual desire. Many of the photos featured individual shots, of various women, various ethnicities, and almost all of them in semi-nude poses, sprawled across a couch. Just as he mastered the art of manipulating criminals to do a good portion of his dirty work, Campbell was able to talk the clothes right off a bevy of his favorite beauties.

Similar to what was found in his own home, investigators removed a large number of miscellaneous items like this from his stash at William's place. The find, again, seemed to suggest Campbell kept the collection almost like trophies. The entire staff of investigators involved now knew his reputation as a paid assassin. That said, and even though this was basically circumstantial evidence, if that even, the find points to a very specific type of individual. One of kind was Chester, yet his methods

– particularly with regard to his interest in murder victims – seemed eerily similar to, or perhaps more associated with the profile generally reserved for serial killers. Definite hints of narcissism. Chester was not a serial killer by any means. He was a professional in the business of underworld enforcement, which obviously included murder. His keeping of mementos and the like was not a wise decision, but did not make him a psychopath in the sense of serial killers. Campbell was never random, and almost always paid for his services. But again, the narcissism element made him appear even more ominous, scary in the eyes of investigators.

And ultimately these "mementos" were the types of items police were indeed looking for, as noted in the request for search warrants. The law wanted to see if Chester Wheeler Campbell kept any keepsakes that could link him to actual crimes.

Also found during the search of Campbell's stash in Mary William's basement were suspected drugs. Corporal Walsh made the discovery. "I found a plastic bag approximately 10" x 10" with a white substance in it," he stated. "This was turned over to Dale Rose of the Oakland County Identification Bureau." Rose was on site specifically for taking and tabulating all the property confiscated during the execution of the search warrant.

Interestingly, the container of questionable powder weighed more than a pound. In terms of drug quantities and street value, this was a lot of dope indeed. Furthermore, as testing would prove the powder was in fact narcotics, cops had found much higher quantity of illicit drugs in William's home than in Chester's. It would seem Campbell felt somewhat at ease hoarding more of the truly damning items, including photographs and news clipping, at his lover's pad than his own. This isn't to say he didn't keep plenty of contraband in his own place, as the searches on Ivanhoe showed he certainly did. Rather, Chester Wheeler Campbell more likely thought his girlfriend's place would simply be an improbable spot for enemies, thieves or cops to look. She was a respected funeral director, and did pretty well for herself financially. He was very wrong, as the latter of those perceived foes proved him with their powerful search warrant.

Investigators searching William's home also took items related to the business she shared with Evelyn Mason. Registration cards for the funeral home's Cadillac's were confiscated, plus numerous receipts, key chains, and other miscellaneous paperwork.

As the information retrieved also indicated that Chester was actually employed, legitimately, by the Mason-Williams Funeral Home, it was apparent he ran errands, drove the vehicles and assisted in various other duties. Even gangsters have to hold down day jobs, at least on paper, for keeping their cover. But Chester Campbell did in fact operate the vehicles registered to Evelyn Mason, for use in the funeral home business she and Chester's girlfriend Mary Williams operated.

All of these materials were taken into custody and added to the mounting evidence file against him. A hit man, a lover and a funeral home, the scenario proves truth is stranger than fiction!

How much did the funeral home proprietors know about Chester Campbell did 'other' business dealings? Suspicious relationships raised red flags, but investigators didn't have enough to go after either woman any further. Campbell, on the other hand, unintentionally gave them plenty of evidence – served on a virtual silver platter, including documentation of his associates and co-conspirators.

The day after both Chester's and Mary's houses were raided, the Intelligence Unit of the Michigan Department of Treasury was called and told of the cash that was confiscated. Promptly, the department issued a jeopardy sales tax assessment totaling $314,304.90. A notice of levy was served on Campbell while he was in the Oakland County jail on March 3. Detroit police officers and the Oakland County Prosecutor's Office handed over $127,775.38 to the Treasury agents. For Chester... this meant war.

CHAPTER THIRTEEN

REVELATIONS OF A HIT MAN

"The oldest and strongest emotion of mankind is fear."
- H.P. Lovecraft

MORE STARTLING DISCOVERIES relating to Campbell were made in the early days of March. Detroit Police Chief Philip Tannian and Coretta Scott King, wife of the late Dr. Martin Luther King Jr. were guest speakers at the Michigan State University for a conference on crime. During the engagement, Chief Tannian made a shocking announcement.

"There was a school for professional hit men in Detroit," he stated, "but it is out of business."

Though he remained reticent when the question of Campbell's recent arrest was raised, Tannian did remark that all but one of the 'school's' pupils were already incarcerated or deceased. For reasons he did not go into, Tannian also refused to offer any further details on the school itself or those who operated and studied within it.

Trying to shift gears quickly, he sharply declared, "We'll hear all about it soon."

Tannian was clearly preventing any pre-trial publicity that might affect the outcomes. To quickly close the subject he said, "There are prosecutions pending."

It's quite reasonable to imagine Tannian's findings all tied into the bizarre complexities of a case so dynamic and large that the very foundation of Detroit's sense of law and order would be shaken. That case of course was the 10th Precinct Conspiracy. Again, he was directly asked if the one remaining alumni was indeed Chester Campbell. Until the time was right, his lips were sealed, thus dodging the question altogether. King then took to addressing a general discussion of the city's crime problems for the remainder of the conference.

Oddly enough, the public never did "hear all about it." Neither Chief Tannian nor the media ever truly delved any further into the specifics of this mysterious institute of underworld learning. In a long list of questions without solid answers, yet another one is added.

With no more information on the school, or Chester Wheeler Campbell's relation to it, the story died off. It wasn't long though for Campbell's name to come up for something else.

Just days after Chief Tannian's announcement, Detroit police released another peculiar find from their search of Campbell's home. Although a treasure trove of illegal and unusual items had been confiscated (and tallied up for the press to run wild with) when cops raided his Ivanhoe address shortly after his February 6th arrest, this particular find needed deeper investigation prior to making it a public affair.

Turns out, Chester had an authentic police badge and complete uniform stashed at his home. Detroit authorities traced all the items back to a police department in Ohio.

Detroit investigators contacted Toledo police regarding the

articles. Records kept by the Toledo department indicated the badge was reported lost, by a former Toledo officer, five years earlier, and the uniform was a type the force discontinued three years prior to the find in Campbell's home. Additionally, the uniform had been stripped of nametags, but a commanding officer's style of hat was present, completing the set of official trousers and short-sleeved shirt.

When the story hit newspapers, Toledo police had not yet determined if the uniform had ever been officially reported as lost or stolen. However, in another perplexing twist, police did divulge how the officer's badge went missing – at least how the incident was originally reported. In his report, the former cop stated he "lost the badge while assisting a disabled motorist."

Chester Wheeler Campbell made trips to Ohio, frequently. Moreover, he was in possession of numerous phony I.D.'s, some of which attested to his being a resident of the 'Buckeye State.' The fake Ohio driver's license, and other forms of identification found during searches of Campbell's property, all signified he lived in Cleveland (though each form of identification displayed differing home addresses within the city). As for his Ohioan alter ego... Chester was known as *Augustus Miller*.

Perhaps the motorist with car troubles, as reported by the former Toledo cop in 1970, was indeed Detroit's infamous hit man. Coincidental? Possibly. Only Chester knew the real story of how that uniform and badge came into his possession. Still, the chronicle of his exploits and skills in the art of manipulation up to this point certainly make such a scenario more than reasonable. Moreover, this was the first sign indicating that Campbell didn't limit his alter egos to fake I.D.'s, but he also had grown accustomed to donning disguises. This was not a typical criminal, not even in the unpredictable and scandalous underworld of Detroit.

The first week of March had yet another foreboding, albeit vague revelation. Publicly, the move was little noticed, but officials in three counties were extremely concerned about newly revealed threats, and took quick action. Information had been obtained regarding a plot to kidnap at least four judges. On the evening of Tuesday March 4, within a few hours following Chief Philip Tannian's comments at the crime conference, a report was passed around law enforcement offices, alerting police of the alleged scheme. Cops were unsure of the validity or where the information originated, but followed protocol by placing a net of extra security around the four judges mentioned plus all twenty of Detroit's Recorder's Court judges. The only information police were sure of... the plot had something to do with Chester Wheeler Campbell, who was currently still being held in Oakland County Jail in Pontiac Michigan.

Judge Alice Gilbert was the first one called. "One day when this matter was pending, a got a call from the Sheriff of a neighboring county and he told me he had come across a plot, from some inmates in the county jail that he found reliable, discussing kidnapping me to secure the release of Chester Campbell." The tough judge wasn't the type to run and hide, but she was very angry at the media's handling of the news.

"I was a little upset the next morning because the television news was talking about the kidnapping of a judge to secure the release of a prisoner, but they didn't say my name. It was me they were talking about, though they didn't say my name, and I thought any nut that hears that will get the idea to do it. I wasn't too happy about that."

Chester's ability to instill fear in others was seemingly inescapable, even while he was incarcerated. The notebooks, no doubt, were the basis of many security risks. Of the many names listed in his prized documentation, the one's of those still alive that is, prosecutors, cops and judges were among them. The problem for law enforcement was sorting out what lists were individuals "on the take" and those considered "targets."

Judge Gilbert however was not easily intimidated, though she says she certainly believed Campbell was a very dangerous individual. She recalls how the situation further developed saying, "The County Sheriff informed me he would assign a deputy to my house, but I said, "What good would that do? If this guy wants to get you – he'll get you." She kept her dry sense of humor throughout the whole ordeal. "He'll have somebody get you someplace, so I refused that offer. I told the sheriff whoever comes to kidnap me – I hope they give me a few moments to pack a few things because you know a gal needs a few things."

Nevertheless, as a mother of two children, Gilbert says her safety concerns were for the kids. So, for several weeks, she had them ride the school bus to friend's homes for fear they could be kidnapped at her house. "I wouldn't allow my children to come on the school bus until I was in the house," explains Judge Gilbert. "I took precautions that way."

And then in April, while things were looking quite bleak for the alleged hit man, Chester and his crack team of attorney's thought they'd received some wonderful news. Recorder's Court Judge Donald Leonard ruled that police illegally confiscated the $280,100 bounty found in Campbell's home during the raid. The warrant issued, as the judge addressed, only stated search and seizure of weapons, drugs and documents. Judge Leonard's decision would not, however, bring any tangible relief to Campbell.

Campbell's fiery attorney Elbert Hatchett said in response,

"The police do this to harass the people they arrest because they know how hard it is to get money back when the IRS gets it." Hatchett wasn't incorrect in his worry that Campbell would never see the cash again. The government did take it all and his client would wind up fighting for its return for another decade.

"They know they can't keep it," Hatchett proclaimed to the press, "so they call the IRS and tell them they're welcome to all the money." The Treasury Department and Internal Revenue Service took every penny.

CHAPTER FOURTEEN

SCANDAL OF THE CENTURY

"Judges, lawyers and politicians have a license to steal. We don't need one."

– Carlo Gambino

WHAT PHILIP TANNIAN was so concerned about, during his very brief announcement regarding a school for hit men in early March 1975, was the upcoming trial of the century for Detroit. Tannian didn't want to even remotely jeopardize the massive prosecutions going down in Recorders Court in the summer of 1975. Hence his vague and non-explanatory responses to questions about Chester Wheeler Campbell and this alleged school. It was the culmination of over three years investigative work, but the conspiracy case involving dirty cops and underworld allies was finally commencing.

Kingpin Henry Marzette's story was far from being the only instance of a cop jumping ship. The drug trade stood so lucrative by the dawn of 1970 that an entire police precinct came under investigation for actually being a critical element in the business's success. The difference between Marzette and the lawmen of the infamous 10th Precinct on Livernois in West Detroit… Henry had not worn the 'blue' for quite some time in his efforts to rule the heroin trade. Those in question from the 10th Precinct were all very much active duty boys in blue.

The Motor City was about to learn the subversive stories surrounding the conspiracy's main characters, like Milton "Happy" Battle, Rudy Davis, and Richard Herold. The public would also hear about barbaric and salacious activities as detailed from star witnesses, which included former drug users, dealers and associates like the prostitute Peaches Miles and enforcer Wiley Reed. More importantly though, the truth was going to come out about a loosely organized, but far reaching stretch of corruption that spread from the halls of justice through the west side of Detroit like a plague. An entire police precinct went awry. Rogue cops, sanctioned dope houses, territory fights, prostitution, torture, castration and of course murder were just some of affairs under the nose of, or directly sanctioned by employees of Detroit's 10th Precinct.

This situation – what would become Detroit's longest running and most expensive courtroom drama – had cops on the take, cops obstructing justice, cops doing favors and of course – cops selling drugs themselves. The scandal became known by two names: Pingree Street Conspiracy and The 10th Precinct Conspiracy. While Chester Wheeler Campbell was most definitely a participant in this underworld expanse of corruption, the sprawling case was far greater than any of its individual players, demonstrating just how widespread the drug problem in Detroit had evolved. His now infamous notebook collection had more than a few pages dedicated to the top cop in charge of investigating all the corruption, and where witnesses were being protected.

To put the whole conspiracy in perspective, and sort out the twisted plotline of an almost unfathomable street drama, well that was resting on the ability of Recorder's Court Judge Justin Ravitz. His work was cut out for him, to say the least.

If the 10th Precinct was essentially mission command for the thriving narcotics business from 1970 through 1973, as a two year long investigation seemed to reveal, then the ill-reputed "Pingree Street" was ground zero in a larger area that was largely littered with dealer safe houses, drug dens and plenty of prostitution. This area was where the real down and dirty business took place, and it looked like everybody was on the take.

This stretch of road is less than three miles from the 10th Precinct building, yet was home to almost every conceivable criminal element. Hookers, pushers, rival dealers, dirty cops and even a snitch or two all gravitated to, or already lived on or near Pingree. Also a familiar name and presence in the scene was none other than Chester Wheeler Campbell.

An individual with the tenacity, skill and willingness, such that Campbell imbued, was both respectable and highly desirable in the underworld. Historically a crucial part of any organized crime structure was, naturally, an enforcement element. That job needed to be filled by someone who could easily instill fear or persuasion, plus the talent and trustworthiness to carry out duties, even if calling for the most severe form of punishment. Chester Wheeler Campbell was indeed that type of person. When other 'enforcers' turned informant, or simply didn't pull their weight, Campbell was called to duty. He instilled fear in other killers as much as he did with any other contract target.

His name circulated the area from Livernois to Pingree to Oakland and beyond. The reputation was not limited within criminal sets either. Law enforcement was beginning to catch on to Campbell's rising status within the underworld culture. As the truth of Chester Campbell's reputation developed in more detail, it became clear this man had associations and transactions with every conceivable type of persons, including business owners, lawyers, prostitutes, and mobsters.

The man behind the investigation of the 10th Precinct was a determined black cop named George Bennett. Tenacious and unwavering in the face of increasing animosity for his efforts, Bennett dedicated every available resource to root out the bad elements tainting the police force upon receipt of solid tips that something very bad was at work on Livernois. Bennett was prominently listed in Campbell's notes, details including the man's family situation, where he met with informants and where he was possibly hiding those informants and witnesses.

Bennett's efforts eventually lead to the arrests of cops, pushers and thugs. By May of 1973, a citizen's grand jury indicted twelve police officers and sixteen civilians. Although twenty-eight people were originally indicted, the actual number was reduced to sixteen when all was said and done. It took roughly two years of very secretive police work for Bennett and his equally cloistered team of three officers, known as the "318" unit, to crack the conspiracy which began to reveal itself during the dope wars of 1970 through 1972. The early testimony revealed much in way of the *who, what, where and when* regarding Detroit's monstrous heroin problems. His investigation was, some said, kicked off by the undercover work of reporter Howard Kohn. Disguised as any other street dweller, Kohn gathered information on Detroit's drug underworld and the cops who were taking payoffs or engaging in deals directly. Bennett took those tips and began a war of his own, trying to bring down the whole department.

Chester Wheeler Campbell's role would never be fully explored once the trial got underway in July. On Friday, February

28th, just days before Chief of Police Philip Tannian uttered the startling news of trained assassins in the city, Chester was being officially dropped from the Conspiracy case. Instead of putting Campbell in the already convoluted conspiracy trial, prosecutors decided to charge him with intent to murder a witness in the case. Wayne County prosecutors made their decision after Judge Robert B. Webster in Oakland County Circuit Court arraigned Campbell on the gun and drug charges.

By now, the Wayne County Organized Crime Unit had raided Campbell's home, Oakland County authorities had done the same at Mary Williams' place, and upon all the relevant findings felt confident in going after him for more direct crimes. The unit was also on the hunt for Campbell's associate Leroy "Bang Bang" James. The pair was charged with attempted murder of Wiley Reed – one of the conspiracy trial's star witnesses. James, however, was nowhere to be found, so Chester Campbell was priority number one.

The significance of Reed's testimony was immeasurable. This guy was giving up deep secrets on a multitude of Detroit's major and minor drug dealers. If he was believed, Reed had knowledge of virtually everyone who was anyone in the drug business from the late sixties to early seventies. Many figures in the drug underworld wanted him dead.

One of the other primary subjects of the Pingree investigation was Milton "Happy" Battle. In an ongoing series of reports that detailed the conspiracy trial, Ann Arbor Sun staffer Pamela Johnson explained "Happy" Battle as "a good looking black man" who, in 1969, paid a visit to Guido Iaconelli – a functionally illiterate, proprietor of a small repair shop in Farmington Michigan. A relationship was forged that would change the engine repairman's life forever. An association based on narcotics business was born.

Johnson's coverage of the trial was unmitigated, colorful, detailed, but more or less the only thorough information available to a news-consuming public. (She minced no words in her articles when it came to that fact; she frequently "called out" the major news media outlets for not reporting on this enormous conspiracy.)

The purpose of the visit, according to prosecutors, was nothing less than an express effort to form a partnership in crime. Johnson's articles painted a virtual picture of the appointment as one that effectively became a life-changing experience for the Iaconelli. The repairman was, perhaps to his own dismay, not going to slide on a defense of basic ignorance, though many of the original people indicted had already been set free. He was indeed also brought to trial for alleged involvement in the conspiracy, even his wife's heartfelt testimony on his behalf made little difference. Prosecutors were convinced the repairman was a willing, important participant in a large-scale narcotics trafficking conspiracy that was woven into the threads of West Detroit's 10th Precinct police station.

Battle's explanation for meeting Iaconelli, conversely, was simply out of need; to secure a good repairman for his concrete saw and could find nobody in the vicinity to do the work. Of course that's not how the prosecution imagined the scenario and accused Iaconelli of directly assisting in heroin and cocaine trafficking organized by Battle.

When many other original targets of the investigation were eventually dropped from the case (Chester being one of those) Iaconelli found himself firmly positioned within "Pingree Sixteen" that faced the judge and jury in July of 1975. Happy Battle... well, he was considered the civilian 'ace' of the operation, but not the kingpin per se. Furthermore, Battle had offered to testify in return for a lighter sentence. The trial was firmly aimed at another man. That title was reserved for a man named Richard Herold, who had been defined in the media as the late Henry Marzette's protégé. Herold was a cop in the 10th Precinct and had been during the time period of Pingree's drug haven heyday, and the time when Marzette was allegedly Detroit's biggest dope kingpin.

The difference between Marzette and Herold, however diminutive, all came down to the badge. Although Marzette had indeed been involved in drug dealing while in uniform, he didn't come full circle in the game of narcotics until he relinquished any allegiance to the force. Richard Herold, on the other hand, was an active duty cop, was not a trafficker as such, but definitely considered front and center for obstruction of justice, i.e. making sure things went smoothly in the local drug business.

He would try to dismiss the accusations as pure political thuggery. Some people even came running to his defense, swearing that Herold was a 'good cop.' Testimony during trial pitted Herold squarely against Bennett in a no holds barred showdown. The weapons in this epic battle were the proverbial 'he said – she said' formula of hearsay.

Herold told the court how George Bennett wanted to take down everyone from the bottom to the top of the police hierarchy. Herold went so far as testifying that Bennett – himself wearing a price tag - was considering hiring a hit man to take out top cops involved. George Bennett remained composed, but not everyone saw him as 'angelic' in his efforts to root out the dope connection in West Detroit.

Again, the truth was only really known by those parties involved. Nonetheless, by July of 1975 Judge Ravitz and the jury were listening to, and sorting through, derisive testimony of alleged conversations involving blackmail, assault and murder plots between a cop on the take and a cop on the hunt that had been ongoing since 1970, if not earlier.

Even if Richard Herold was the understudy of the late Henry Marzette, the trial would turn a greater focus on another 10th Precinct cop – Sergeant Rudy Davis. Much of the banter exchanged in court revealed that Rudy Davis – a white cop - was most likely the real figure behind the conspiracy, or at least that's how Herold described it.

Basically the entire case was filled with verbal warfare from witnesses, attorneys and the accused. Herold further painted a picture of Bennett in much less glorious or righteous manner, saying the cop just wanted to destroy Rudy Davis by any means necessary. In that cause, purely political as described by Herold's testimony, Bennett would do whatever it took to take down Davis – hence the alleged discussion of a professional 'hit' if necessary. Testimony was taking this drama to new lows, a place where everyone was accused of very dirty deeds – including the so-called 'good guys' of law and order.

Some defense witnesses, including a few addicts and prostitutes who roamed the Pingree area, characterized the cops of the '318' as bullies, armed with threats to get information. It seemed nobody involved in the conspiracy case was completely upstanding. The former prostitute, Peaches Miles, wept on the stand when she related tales of repeated bullying by one of Bennett's 318 cops. This was never a cut and dry case.

The trial went on for the remainder of 1975, finally reaching a close in December. Many of the original defendants were dropped over time. Some turned witness, a few died, and only a handful of the sixteen defendants were convicted. A few, such as Richard Herold, took to legal motions for years trying to reverse his conviction. Overall, the 10th Precinct Conspiracy investigation did not impede the progress of an incredibly lucrative drug trade in Detroit. Ultimately, the arrests, trials and discoveries that came out of the whole experience did little or nothing to curb the drug addiction problem of Detroit either.dsf

And as for the *hit man school* that Police Chief Philip Tannian spoke of… there were plenty of assassins and enforcers roaming both East and West Detroit from 1970 to 1975. Although the 'school' itself was not directly identified during the conspiracy trial, surely, if there had been a place where these hit men were taught – the area overseen by the 10th Precinct would be a likely region, and Chester Wheeler Campbell, among others, graduates or teachers themselves. Once word was out that investigation into the highly lucrative and shady drug trade of West Detroit was underway, well, paranoia begun to run rampant. The result of such 'worry' lead to drastic measures being taken, i.e. contracts were put out on anyone and everyone that someone else feared might implicate them.

Campbell was absolutely a person of interest when the trial began, but again, he was dropped just before commencement. The evidence against him was loose at best. But more pressing was the issue of Campbell's bullying witnesses involved with the trial. If the law didn't have the evidence, or time, to include him directly in the Pingree/10th Precinct proceedings… that was fine because Campbell was under the gun for an array of other criminal investigations. One way or another, Campbell was going to face a judge and jury.

CHAPTER FIFTEEN

DRAMA OF A HIT MAN

"It is the trade of lawyers to question everything, yield nothing, and talk by the hour."
– Thomas Jefferson

AS IF THERE weren't enough legal phenomena already ever-present in Detroit, outlandish courtroom antics were about to become the norm in the summer of 1975. Scandal, rumors and conspiracy were not limited to the criminal element either. This constant turn of events was not helping to law's efforts to put Chester Wheeler Campbell away. Good guys were under scrutiny for doing some not-so-good things and the bad guys were being testified against by, well, basically just a bunch of other bad guys.

What happens when all of those elements come together? In Detroit's sultry summer months… it equaled pandemonium in the court. There were more arguments, physical altercations, threats and displays of disrespect and courtroom theatrics than any scripted television drama could've ever come up with.

Campbell, known as one who usually conducted himself pro-

fessionally in any situation, was beginning a trend of verbal com-
bativeness in court, and his attorneys weren't any better behaved.
Particularly Elbert Hatchett and co-counsel Wilfrid Rice. The
flamboyant pair was well versed in the laws, and it's grey areas,
but in Courtroom Theater – they put on a show worthy of charging admission. These two knew Chester Campbell perhaps better
than anybody, as demonstrated back during their February appearance before Judge Webster.

With his removal from the gargantuan 10th Precinct/Pingree
Street conspiracy case, Campbell was spared one ordeal, but
dealt even more bad cards. His legal team, however, saw potential. Hatchett displayed great confidence, exuberance and show-
manship in Judge Robert Webster's courtroom, where Chester
Campbell was being tried on the three counts of carrying a concealed weapon and one count of heroin possession. Webster was
all too familiar with Chester Campbell and his team of attorneys.

The trial was not in the Motor City, not even in Wayne County. The trial was not in held in Oakland County where the Orchard Lake arrest took place. Not going to happen, at least not
if Campbell's lawyers had anything to say about it. And they did
have a lot to say.

Chester Wheeler Campbell's attorney Elbert Hatchett knew
there would be slim chance of a fair trial in the predominantly white area of Oakland County, not to mention the fact that
Campbell's arrest made headlines, so the publicity would be
damaging. Originally, trial was to be held in Pontiac, Michigan. A jury of nine women and three men, all white, was not
in Campbell's best interest, so Hatchett requested a different
venue, was granted the move, and the trial was moved to court
in Kalamazoo, approximately 145 miles west of Detroit. Still,
Kalamazoo was also a predominantly white area of the state. The

defense team and prosecutor's office agreed, in an effort to limit the possibility of a trial by media, to the area because it was far west of the location where Campbell had been arrested on drug and weapons charges.

During the course of testimony, in the early days of June, one chaotic incident led to another. Campbell's attorneys were against at odds with their old foe from the Prosecutor's Office – Richard Thompson. First, while on the witness stand, Orchard Lake police officer Corporal John Walsh was questioned by Campbell's attorney Elbert Hatchett. Walsh was reading a document to jog his memory when Hatchett stormed the stand. "Let me see that," he demanded, and then seized the piece of paper from Walsh's hands. He swiftly handed the file over to Rice. The bold move caused Oakland County Assistant Prosecutor Richard Thompson to verbally condemn Hatchett's action, and followed the statement by snatching the document from Wilfrid Rice's hands.

Rice, (reportedly once a military boxing champ and black belt in the martial arts) a much larger man than the prosecutor, took hold of Thompson by the shoulders and angrily warned, "Don't you every snatch something out of my hand that way." Others quickly separated the two opposing attorneys in the courtroom, mostly members of the prosecution staff, while Campbell and Hatchett looked on.

Judge Webster tried to bring order to the courtroom, condemning the juvenile actions of both sides. Because Campbell's counsel still felt they would not get a fair trial with an all-white jury, only Judge Webster was hearing the case. Campbell waived his right to trial by jury before the case began. If there had been a jury present, they would have been in for more of a show.

Just after order was restored, Elbert Hatchett began voicing his disdain for the number of weapons visible in the courtroom.

He told the judge he could not continue, "In this atmosphere of oppression." He was furious over members of the prosecutor's staff carrying handguns. He loudly chastised stating," All those men with guns come up here and put their hands on my co-counsel – not one of them touched Mr. Thompson. I can't continue this trial with all those guns behind my back."

The Judge went on to call out all those present who were carrying firearms. A total of eight people in the courtroom stood, including prosecution staffers, witnesses and deputies. Judge Webster conceded to Hatchett's request and ejected all but the two deputies from court that day. The other six were told not to return to court unless they surrender their weapons. The trial continued, relatively uninterrupted.

Sporting a white fedora, black suit, goatee, and toothpick pressed between his lips, Chester strolled into the court, passed a throng of reporters and photographers, steely eyed, confident, and ready for war. His team of attorneys flanking him, they stood defiantly before Judge Robert Webster in the last week of June, 1975.

Judge Webster took all the evidence, testimony and cross-examinations into account, but even Campbell's fiery team of lawyers couldn't sway the inevitable opinion laid out. Webster found Chester Wheeler Campbell guilty on three counts of carrying a concealed weapon and one count of heroin possession. Attorneys Hatchett and Rice were dead set on filing appeals, but a light sentence down the road was all Campbell could hope for with regard to the Orchard Lake fallout. His focus was quickly adjusted to the charges he was facing for the 1972 murder of Roy J. Parsons. Authorities in Detroit were anxious to get the trial underway.

Less than two weeks following his appearance in Kalamazoo on weapons and drug charges, Campbell was shipped back to

Detroit to face the murder charge. He was not alone this time. Also charged in the Parsons murder were Donald Johnson and Charles P. Loukas. Back in early March, while Chester was being held without bond in Oakland County Jail, Detroit's Recorders Court Judge George W. Campbell ordered the three to trial: Chester for first-degree murder and inducement to murder, the other two for first-degree murder. The key witness against the trio of assassins was James Lee Newton, commonly known on the streets by the nickname "Watusi Slim". Presiding over the actual trial was a contentious Judge named James Del Rio.

The gun toting Del Rio had a controversial history, which included three marriages, as many divorces, and rumors of having never practiced law until his election to the bench. The judge had even been shot at – during a trial in 1972 – by a gun waving defense attorney. It happened to be a day when the Judge wasn't carrying his handgun under the robes (because he had been under scrutiny for that issue as well). The situation ended when the attorney turned the gun on himself, placing a bullet in his own head, right in the middle of the courtroom. With that sort of past, Del Rio was accustomed to tough detractors - not a man easily intimidated, not even by the Motor City's most notorious enforcer. Nevertheless, he was being overwhelmed by an ongoing investigation into his own judicial practices.

On June 10th, a preliminary hearing with Watusi Slim revealed conflicting testimony. Slim testified that Chester Campbell paid him $500 for luring Roy Parsons into a waiting vehicle. Once Parsons was in the car, he said one of the passengers – either Loukas or Johnson – fired a gun and killed Parsons instantly. Slim made it clear to the court that Chester Wheeler Campbell was not present at the murder scene, and he was not sure who fired the deadly shot. Slim, a career criminal himself, also made it known he feared for his own life if he didn't do as Campbell had instructed.

Newton further divulged the entire plot stemmed from an earlier time in 1972 when Campbell and Parsons engaged in a heated argument. The exchange of threats turned violent when Parsons brandished a handgun and blasted Chester in the leg. Parsons fled the scene and Campbell sought medical help. Interestingly, this particular murder was, as Newton characterized it, a 'revenge' hit, which was out of character for the ultra-professional assassin. Then again, Parsons put a bullet in Campbell's lower extremity and that gesture was destined to be reciprocated one way or another. That day arrived for Roy J. Parsons in December of 1972.

However, as the trial was underway, ten witnesses came forward stating that Donald Johnson was in Cleveland on the date of the murder, thereby putting Slim's statements in question. Campbell's defense team cried foul and Judge Del Rio quickly postponed the trial. The prosecution had based most of their case on James Lee " Watusi Slim" Newton's testimony, and this revelation was going set Johnson free, possibly Campbell and Loukas as well.

The situation then morphed into a more bizarre, ultra racist and fear-inducing nightmare for Judge Del Rio. The news of Campbell's trial postponement, added to the widely known issues Del Rio was having because of inquiries into alleged 'back room' deals, apparently made a few anonymous entities quite worried. The reason for panic? That Campbell would go free, as Del Rio was already under scrutiny, by the Michigan Judicial Tenure Commission, for making deals to lessen sentences – behind closed doors and without the knowledge of prosecutors. These unidentified enemies of Judge Del Rio (and obviously

Chester Wheeler Campbell) took to methods of intimidation that harkened back to the age of "Black Hand" mobsters of the early twentieth-century.

Before the infamous mobster Charles Lucky Luciano and his colleagues 'organized and modernized' the New York mafia in 1931, the old school "Moustache Petes" or "Black Hand" criminals would prey on those within their own neighborhoods, usually demanding cash payoffs with promised bodily harm if requests were not met. These threats, initiated usually by letter, were often signed by a black handprint or scribbled images of knives and blood -rudimentary and difficult to trace. Unlike the predecessors of the contemporary mafia though, Del Rio's shadowy enemies were not after money. They certainly did send the anonymous threatening letter though. There was no handprint, but rather a more direct a message of racist intimidation. The letter to Del Rio was signed with a swastika symbol.

Judge James Del Rio also received a follow-up phone call from someone claiming to be the issuer of the threatening note. "The man said they would take a double-barrel shotgun and blow my head off if Chester Campbell was found innocent by me or a jury," Del Rio told the press.

The ominous memo was also shown to the media. It's closing remarks read, "*We are waiting for the right moment – Waffen S.S.*"

When the trial continued, Del Rio disclosed the threat in open court. He asked both the prosecution and defense attorneys if they wanted to disqualify him from the case in light of the terrorizations. The attorneys for Campbell, Loukas and Johnson, however, asked Del Rio to remain on the case.

Then, another one of Detroit's prominent black attorneys, Milton Henry, came forward just after the Del Rio incident and said he was told the threats against the judge came directly from the DPOA – Detroit Police Officers Association. Henry believed the organization planned to assassinate the judge. The DPOA brushed off the allegations, saying Henry and Del Rio were merely after some publicity. Still, the thought of Chester Wheeler Campbell walking the streets of Detroit a free man was obviously making some people very nervous.

The trial went on. Even with the perjury issue raised upon James Lee Newton's testimony, Chester Campbell realized this witness was still the only thing standing in his way of acquittal in the case. James Lee "Watusi Slim" Newton was the sole eyewitness talking, so ideally, if he was silenced – Chester would no longer have this particular thorn in his side. Campbell's wish was about to come true.

CHAPTER SIXTEEN

SUMMER OF 75

"Where justice is denied, where poverty is enforced, where igno-rance prevails, and where any one class is made to feel that society is an organized conspiracy to oppress, rob and degrade them, neither persons nor property will be safe."
- Frederick Douglass

WHILE CHESTER FACED a mass of legal troubles, the city of Detroit was again on a troubling path of its own. In July, a riot broke out on the corner of Livernois and Chalfonte Avenue. This heated explosion of angst did not reach the level of the 1967 riot, but it was no less devastating to those involved. The location of ground zero for the unrest was Bob Bolton's Bar and Grill, a white owned establishment. Although differing accounts were told of what exactly started the events, race was certainly brought into the discussion. Andrew Chinar-ian, the bar's owner, allegedly took matters into his own hands upon witnessing three black youths tampering with his vehicle. He shot and killed one of the youths, eighteen-year-old Obie Wynn. Some witnesses claimed Chinarian chased after a fleeing Wynn, while others believed Wynn was approaching Chinarian. Whatever the case may have been, all hell broke loose in the area just south of Fenkell Avenue, and so the riot was forever known as the Livernois-Fenkell Riot.

Making matters worse, word had spread that Bolton's only served white patrons, and then Chinarian – upon arrest – was held on a very low bond. Rioters in response subsequently ransacked the bar. Mayor Coleman Young eventually helped diffuse the situation, but not before fifty arrests, thousands of dollars in damage to local businesses and the death of fifty-four year old concentration camp survivor Marian Pyszko. The bakery worker was on his way home from the job when rioters pulled him from his car and beat him to death with a piece of concrete. One of those arrested – and later acquitted – was a co-founding member of the soon-to-be infamous drug gang Young Boys Inc., an organization that became notorious beginning in the late 1970's and into the 80's.

The summer was only getting hotter. An uprising was calmed in the black community, but by no means was everything okay. Unemployment was causing people to take drastic measures, and drug use of course was only getting worse. Middle class citizens were feeling financial pain, and the poor were becoming poorer. As for outlaws, the dealers in West Detroit who hadn't been indicted by, or turned witness for, the Pingree Conspiracy trial were still at work, raking in the illicit cash. Drug lords in East Detroit were going full steam ahead in their business. The mafia was rather busy as well. Even though black drug lords had taken a good chunk of their market share in narcotics away, mob traffickers were still able supply black dealers who remained loyal. The heroin trade was, for all intent and purpose, going strong despite the 10th Precinct/Pingree trial. But the mob was also busy in the lucrative labor racket, particularly with Teamsters boss Jimmy Hoffa. This relationship would culminate in the most legendary,

still unsolved mystery of the twentieth century. July 30th, 1975…
the day Hoffa disappeared.

Located on Telegraph Road in Bloomfield Hills, the Machus
Red Fox Restaurant was a little over seven miles south from
where Chester Wheeler Campbell almost sideswiped a Keego
Harbor cop in February. The charming and generally undis-
ruptive region where Campbell made those shocking headlines
was yet again destined for bizarre happenings. This time however, the incident would prove to be an even greater gangland
legend, endemic with mystery that would basically overshadow
and outlast even the formidable reputation and legal drama of
Chester Campbell.

James Riddle Hoffa was expecting to meet two men, for lunch,
at the establishment on Telegraph Road in on July 30th. The former Teamster boss agreed to a meeting with former New Jersey Teamsters Vice President Anthony "Tony Pro" Provenzano
– with whom he had dispute – and Detroit mobster Anthony
"Tony Jack" Giacalone. "Tony Jack" was supposed to serve as a
mediator of sorts. The meeting was scheduled for 2:00 pm, and
Hoffa was a very punctual type. He arrived one half-hour early.
At two sharp, he was still alone. Fifteen minutes went by and
still no show for the either of the men. Hoffa, sporting blue shirt,
slacks, black Gucci loafers, made his way to a nearby payphone
and let his wife know he had been stood up. He was last seen,
just minutes following the phone call to his wife, in the back seat
of a maroon 1975 Mercury Marquis Brougham. The witness, a
truck driver, claimed he recognized Hoffa in the car with other
unknown men and a long item covered by a blanket – which
he claimed looked a lot like the shape of a gun. As legend, and
investigations confirm, that was the last anyone (who was willing
to talk) ever heard from or saw him.

The FBI was brought in on the case within days of disappearance. Few people thought anything less than foul play was involved, as Hoffa was the most iconic – and polarizing – character of American union politics and history. But his long relationship with mafia factions had both served his needs and stirred bad blood over time. The mob was not very interested in Hoffa's presumed attempt to regain control. Provenzano was certainly one of those vocally opposed, and he was a member of the Genovese crime family.

Both Giacalone and Provenzano had alibis for their whereabouts on July 30th. Tony Jack was at the gym and Tony Pro was in Jersey playing cards. However, investigators did find the Mercury. The car belonged to Joseph Giacalone, mobster Tony Jack's son. Police questioned Joe Giacalone about the vehicle, to which he said the car was loaned to long-time friend of Hoffa's named Chuckie O'Brien. He indeed did have the Mercury, but O'Brien told police he was delivering frozen salmon to another Teamster Vice President's wife, afterwards helping her cut the fish up into steaks during the time frame in question. O'Brien's story seemed odd after he also mentioned the salmon leaked blood in the vehicle, and he of course had to clean the mess up because he couldn't give the Mercury back to Joe Giacalone in such a condition. Furthermore, O'Brien's relationship with Hoffa was almost a father-son sort. Hoffa had basically taken him in following his own father's death. Investigators and theorists alike believed it was possible Hoffa would have entered Giacalone's Mercury – without force – because O'Brien was a trusted friend.

Police dogs were brought in, given some of Hoffa's clothing to gain a scent. The canine team was then used to sniff out the interior of Giacalone's Mercury. There was scent found in the back seat and trunk area, but as the old saying goes, "no body, no crime," so little more could be done from that point on. The rumors, conspiracies and wild goose chases of leads would go on for decades, but no Hoffa to be found. The case understandably trumped most of the other Detroit news in the summer months of 1975, including Chester's numerous court cases and the 10th Precinct Conspiracy trial. Hence, part of the reason a man like Chester Wheeler Campbell was not more widely known to the news consuming public.

Detroit police and Federal agents continued the preoccupation with finding Hoffa while Detroit Recorder's court judges dealt with the issue of Chester Wheeler Campbell and trials of cops and drug peddlers from the Pingree conspiracies. The Motor City and surrounding areas were fully engrossed in possibly the most peculiar year of events ever endured.

These incidents had certainly distracted the media and police from Chester Wheeler Campbell. In fact, by the end of July 1975 Campbell's name was barely mentioned again in the press. His story was far from over though, and his presence was not entirely dismissed by any means, not by the judges and prosecutors already knee deep in figuring out how many crimes he was actually responsible for.

And so, Chester Wheeler Campbell found himself in more difficulty, which seemed to be assaulting him from every angle as the months passed. By the time the 10th Precinct Conspiracy Trial finally went before the jury in July, Campbell had been indicted for inducement to murder and jailed on unrelated drugs and weapons violations.

That wasn't all Campbell had to contend with. Authorities had been putting together a stronger case against him in the Roy Parsons murder of 1972. The star witness, James Lee "Watusi Slim" Newton was in prison, holed up in an Ohio Penitentiary, readying himself for an eventual court date to talk all about Chester's well-thought strategy to have Parsons assassinated. Before Campbell's trial on those charges commenced, he was faced with yet another star witness – this one was involved in the 10th Precinct case.

Wiley Reed. He was a thirty-three year old recovering heroin addict and admitted enforcer for some of the people accused in the conspiracy trial, including Milton "Happy" Battle. Reed was particularly recognizable in court. He had come to testify adorned in bandages. In one of the seven or so attempts made on his life, carried out by various perpetrators since he began talking to authorities in the early 1970's, a shotgun blast succeeded in taking a portion of his face off. Notwithstanding the obvious danger involved in offering his testimony for prosecutors, Reed sung like a bird. He took the stand detailing the work he did in the Pingree area, the people he performed duties for, and how much he earned. Reed also described the frequent of attempts on his life, which included multiple shootings and even evading hand grenades that were lobbed at him.

Moreover, Reed did just as his enemies feared – he told the scandalous tales of virtually every dope dealer to operate in Detroit since 1969. In April of 1974, Reed first began spilling the beans when he testified before a Grand Jury. Prosecutor Roy C. Hayes wasted no time in asking Reed what he knew of Detroit's narcotics business. Reed named the people, places and things they were doing. He discussed dealers such as Jesse James, Sweat Pea Malone, Demetrius Baily and even a clothing store owner – Irv Scholnick – who not only sold them fur coats, but also spent a good amount of social time with them. Reed gave addresses and dates, prices and quantities. Reed left no stone unturned throughout Hayes's line of questioning, particularly when asked to recall specific drug exchanges he witnessed and what kind of narcotics the dealers were partial to.

Hayes: *What kind of narcotics are we talking about?*
Reed: *Heroin and cocaine.*
Hayes: *How would Mr. James sell this?*
Reed: *He'd sell it… you had to buy so much. You could buy…one hundred dollars for a quarter spoon of it.*
Hayes: *Was that dope that was sold heroin or cocaine?*
Reed: *It was both.*
Hayes: *It was a mixture?*
Reed: *Yes.*
Hayes: *Do you know how many spoons?*
Reed: *No, I don't*
Hayes: *Did you ever see Mr. James sell any other dope?*
Reed: *No, nothing other than cocaine and heroin.*

Hayes wanted the jury to fully understand the lingo used within the drug business, and how the substances were distributed. He questioned Reed on meanings of specific lingo:

Hayes: *What does it mean when somebody says, "What did the dope take?" Or, "How many cuts?"*

Reed: *Well, this was supposed to be pure and sometimes it would take three, four, five or seven, on how many cuts.*

Perhaps the most revealing information Reed gave, in terms of supply to major dealers, came in his testimony regarding Jesse James's jailhouse associations.

Hayes: *What did Mr. James tell you about where he got the narcotics?*

Reed: *He was telling me while he was in the Federal Institution that he met one of the Genoveses, and this is where the dope was coming from.*

Reed had testified that dealer Jesse James met a member of

New York's Genovese crime family and established a direct line of narcotics supply through that relationship.

Hayes: How would Mr. James receive the narcotics from New York?

Reed: He would have a lady – I can't think of her name – she would leave on a flight before he would, with the money, and they would meet somewhere in New York. And they would either come back through the City Airport or drive, bring the drugs back. When the dope got back to Detroit, he would go on a street called Peter Hunt.

Hayes probed further into who was ultimately responsible for distributing drugs to other dealers. Reed answered almost always, "Jesse James." Then the prosecutor revisited the supply route issue again.

Hayes: Earlier you stated that Mr. James stated that he got his narcotics connection from someone he was in prison with?

Reed: Yes.

Hayes: What was that person's name?

Reed: Genovese.

Hayes: What did Mr. James say concerning that person?

Reed: Said that he was in Leavenworth. And him and Genovese was, shared a cell together while he was there. And this is how he got this dope connection.

Wiley Reed's testimony pointed directly at the infamous crime boss Vito Genovese as the main supplier of heroin and cocaine to wholesale distributors and dealers in Detroit's drug market. In fact, Genovese was the mobster who officially began his leadership after Charles "Lucky" Luciano was exiled to Italy. The once-second-in-command Genovese refashioned the Luciano Family into his own vision, thus it was then named for Genovese. Vito was convicted in 1959 for narcotics, and as Reed testified, was in Leavenworth Prison until January 1969 when health issues – a massive heart attack – prompted his transfer to a medical facility in Missouri. Genovese died two weeks later. But the information that he shared a cell with the dealer known as Jesse James and helped set up a pipeline of dope distribution was an amazing revelation. For years authorities new dope was coming from New York, and that the Mafia was behind most or all of it until people like Henry Marzette established their own sources. Now, with this testimony, it was very apparent that the Italian Mafia was still providing at least some of the major black dealers with large quantities of wholesale drugs. The man who shared a cell with the infamous Vito Genovese, Detroit's Jesse James, had a history of his own. He was also one of the original twenty-eight civilians named in the big conspiracy indictment, yet was never actually brought to court.... The dealer had fled the country once he got wind of the large-scale indictments being handed down, just a few months after Wiley Reed's Grand Jury Testimony. Eventually he returned to the Motor City and the law was patiently waiting. It wasn't the drugs, or the Pingree conspiracy that sealed his fate though. James, like Chester Campbell, took a hit from the tax collector. In March of 1975, James was silent as the judge issued a $50,000 bond. He was found guilty of evading the Federal Government of $400,000 in back taxes over a five-year period, based off an estimated income that reached almost $800,000 in that time. This was large scale and very serious in terms of how far the reach of Detroit's drug lords and mobsters extended. Roy Hayes felt confident in what the Grand Jury had heard. He had one final point to get across, and that was the danger Wiley Reed was in by offering his testimony. Hayes closed the questioning of Reed by asking if he had ever been shot or shot at, to which the witnesses replied affirmatively on all counts. Here was an establishment of Reed's credibility.

It was just this sort of information that required the use of men like Chester Wheeler Campbell, and therefore not surprising the hit man would want to have an actual copy of such a transcript. He and Leroy "Bang Bang" James were named as two of the perpetrators against witness Wiley Reed, but again, they weren't the only ones hired to get Reed in a casket. They were not involved in the incident where Reed's face was disfigured though. Campbell was already incarcerated at the time, and "Bang Bang" James was on the run – presumably laying low in Los Angeles. The man responsible for the shotgun blast that resulted that tore through the left side of Reed's head was named Willie B. Foster. The 1972 attempted murder against Wiley Reed earned Foster a lengthy stay at Michigan State Prison, also known as Jackson Prison – the same prison Chester Wheeler Campbell and so many other Detroit gangsters were all too familiar with. Campbell had, according to his attorney Wilfrid Rice, even worked on a case involving Willie B. Foster. It seemed everyone – dealers, hit men, mobsters, lawyers and addicts included – were all connected directly or loosely in a criminal drama. As the saying goes, it was a very small world after all.

Nevertheless, Campbell's role in the attempted murder of star conspiracy witness Wiley Reed was ongoing, and also being handled in Recorder's Court. Additionally, Chester was still facing charges for the 1972 'revenge' murder of Roy J. Parsons. Just like Wiley Reed, James Lee Newton publicly announced his desire to spill the beans in spectacular detail. The future was not looking very bright for Campbell.

Campbell was going to take a heavy blow if the trend continued. Again, it was already virtually written in stone that Wiley Reed was indeed eagerly relating the specifics of numerous attempts on his life by various would-be assassins – including

Campbell and "Bang Bang" James's role of course.

If it were in Chester's power, both of these men would be put out of commission, permanently. By late August, one of his wishes was granted. In a brazen manner that seemed almost typical and expected throughout the underworld soap opera, one of Campbell's attorneys – Wilfrid Rice (who was also representing one of the accused in the conspiracy case)– marched into the courtroom during a break in the 10th Precinct trial – armed with a cocky announcement for Judge Justin Ravitz and all those present. He loudly broadcast that "Watusi Slim" had been eliminated and the case against Chester Wheeler Campbell dismissed.

"Yes Sir, " Wilfrid Rice proclaimed, "Chester doesn't have to be inside to do business."

Rice's words to the court were both sinister and accurate. Chester Wheeler Campbell, as more than a few testimonials showed, was just as good at manipulating and subcontracting others to carry out deadly deeds. Cleverly, Campbell was very adept in the art of convincing others to do the dirty work.

Newton had been scheduled to be in court within two weeks, promising to offer a large amount of damning testimony. However, on August 21st, Watusi Slim was found dead near the gymnasium area of the Ohio Correctional Facility in Lucasville where he was serving a twenty-five year sentence. His body was sprawled out behind the gymnasium; throat was slashed. However, even that gruesome effect was not enough to make the point, so the perpetrators also carved X's in his eyelids for good measure. From the manner in which Newton's body was left on display, a clear message had been sent to potential 'rats.'

Newton didn't have to be psychic to know his fate was basically spelled out the moment he agreed to testify against Campbell and company. He said as much when asked, during a preliminary hearing, why he was offering testimony. "I figured that they would kill me anyway," he told the court. And so "they" did.

Campbell was being detained in Wayne County Jail when James "Watusi Slim" Newton was brutally murdered. Again, not directly involved, but if his attorney was correct – Chester Wheeler Campbell's deadly reach easily extended beyond prison walls. Strangely, neither the prosecution, nor the defense gave any more credence to Slim's murder having anything to do with Campbell's trial. Twisted irony if there ever was any, but indeed, shortly after the death and Campbell's charges being dropped – public statements from both sides were made saying the murder was unrelated.

What "Watusi Slim" had originally offered prosecutors, in the case of Roy Parson's murder, was a first-person account of *what* happened and *who* was behind the hit. No witness, no case, and no more discussion of it. But, the law was far from finished with Chester. He still had to contend with Wiley Reed, plus all the charges – three counts of carrying a concealed weapon and one count possession of heroin - stemming from his vehicular mishap on Orchard Lake Road back in February.

Chester Wheeler Campbell eventually skated free and clear of three potentially long-term prison sentences. He walked on the 10th Precinct Conspiracy, the Parsons murder investigation and the inducement to murder charge for threatening Wiley Reed. Still being held in jail, Campbell's future remained uncertain. Even with the other charges being dropped, Oakland and Wayne Counties had some very good evidence against him for weapon and drug possession. Worse yet, Campbell's past criminal record was haunting him. Prosecutors were eager to use it against him.

CHAPTER SEVENTEEN

ECONOMICS OF A HIT MAN

"When my ferried seed pops into your hand – and tainted money blossoms from your pocket – I guarantee it won't be the last time,"
– **Anonymous**

THERE IS NO single basic reason for all the bloodshed, conspiracy, and discord that existed. There were many social, economic and cultural reasons. Still, attention can be directed back to the source of all the woes. It was the same core reason for people like Chester Campbell to thrive. Money. Elicit money. Money wasn't growing on trees, but it was coming from a colorfully flowered plant. The economic foundation, of which Chester Wheeler Campbell, Henry Marzette, the mafia, and a bunch of crooked cops blossomed from, particularly from the 1950's through the 1970's, can be traced back to a genus of flora. Opium Poppy. Called a "flower of joy" by the ancient Sumerians, *Papaver somniferum* is the variety of poppy that produces opium. There is a long, sometimes dark history behind the uses of this special plant, but it was the discovery of opium offshoots that changed the world of medicine in the 1800s.

Emergent in arid regions, such as Turkey, Asia, Mexico, the Opium Poppy is hearty, able to withstand droughts longer than many other types of vegetation. It grows in fields; each one with a bulbous top upon a tubular stem, sprouting petals of red or purple. Once the petals fall from the capsule… farmers begin an age-old, labor-intensive process of cultivating a milky sap surrounding the seeds within the bulb. With rudimentary cutting tools, harvesters carve vertical scores into the bulb. As the sap bleeds out, it hardens and turns into a brown paste-like substance. This is opium in its most raw form. The sap is then scraped off and sold or traded. The seeds are collected for planting and other uses. It's the tar-like raw form that has been cleaned and smoked for centuries, giving users a euphoric experience.

However, a 'miracle drug' of sorts was discovered as the first active alkaloid of Opium, in 1804 by Friedrich Sertürner. He called it Morpheum, after the Greek God Morpheus. The name quickly became *Morphine*. A decade later, his company marketed the drug for its extraordinary potential as an elixir, targeting the treatment of alcohol and opium addiction. It wasn't long before they realized morphine was actually far more addictive than alcohol or opium. By the end of the Civil War, hundreds of thousands of veterans were thought to be addicted to morphine, as it was widely used as a painkiller for troops on both sides. This period also saw the advent of the hypodermic needle, which was an amazing tool for more accurate and direct delivery of medicines.

In 1874 things changed again. The Bayer Company discovered Diacetylmorphine, a more powerful derivative. The common name was *heroin*. The work of scientists at Bayer was carried out with the best of intentions. Heroin was thought to be a 'fix' for the problems incurred by morphine use. Of course that was not the eventual result, but as historytoday.com writer Ian Scott explained in his article "Heroin: Hundred Year Habit," there were good outcomes from the synthesizing experiments:

"Now that plant-derived drugs were available in purified form, chemists could modify them to form new molecules that might prove more effective, or perhaps safer to use. In the later 1890s, Dreser and his colleagues adopted this strategy to produce for Bayer two of the most famous drugs in the world today. Heroin, made by adding two acetyl groups to the morphine molecule, was followed a year later by another acetyl derivative of a pain-killer from drugs; the second natural drug was salicylic acid and the Bayer derivative was named 'Aspirin'."

Heroin was sold in the United States for treatment of pain, coughs, colds, cancer, addiction and other ailments. Snake Oil sales pitches were not uncommon, as it was said to cure even old age. From a practical standpoint, the reason for Heroin overtaking Morphine use, besides the misconception that it was non-addictive, had to do with amount and potency. More lipid (fat soluble) than morphine, Heroin requires much smaller doses and is far more effective. The drug enters and impinges on the user's system more quickly as well. It was no surprise the drug became very popular.

"From the late 1800's to the early 1900's the reputable drug companies of the day began manufacturing over-the-counter drug kits. These kits contained a glass barreled hypodermic needle and vials of opiates (morphine or heroin) and/or cocaine packaged neatly in attractive engraved tin cases. Laudanum (opium in an alcohol base) was also a very popular elixir that was used to treat a variety of ills. Laudanum was administered to kids and adults alike - as freely as aspirin is used today." (History of Heroin, NARCONON International)

The unregulated manufacture and sale of Heroin and other

opiate based drugs continued until the early 1900's. The Harrison Narcotics Tax Act of 1914 was put in place to address the marketing of opiates and other drugs, but had considerable loopholes. It wasn't until the British passed the *Dangerous Drug Act* in 1920 and the United States followed in 1922 with the *Narcotics Drug Import and Export Act* that the drug became essentially more illegal. The Brit's version was problematic because it shifted away from the concept of addiction being a disease to something simply punishable. The American view at the time was opium based drugs could still be regulated and issued by doctors under certain conditions.

The government was legitimately concerned with the rising addiction statistics that were beginning to emerge. However, by the time laws were enacted, there was already a thriving market for the substance that surely wouldn't be easily subdued. When there is a demand... there will be suppliers, regardless of legality.

Smack, junk, scag, and "H" are just a few of the numerous slang terms for heroin. Besides various street names, the drug also came if several forms, each of those determined by origin, and most importantly – the chemical process conducted in a lab. The heroin intended for consumers comes in forms for smoking, snorting or injection. The latter of these delivery methods was very popular because it produced the effect much faster than any other method. The manner by which a user consumes the drug is also dependent on the purity (which comes from additional steps in a lab). White heroin, aka number 4, is the purest and is water soluble – ready for injection. Number 3 heroin resembles brown sugar and had gone through fewer purity steps. Users generally smoke this type, or mix it with citric acid in order to liquefy for injection. 1 and 2 are considered 'raw' or 'base' grade heroin. The product that entered the country from Asia was known as

China White, whereas the Mexican heroin was often called *black tar* heroin.

What mafia traffickers did, essentially, was import pure heroin powder into the United States from Southeast Asia, Mexico, Turkey, and so forth. Once the product was successfully smuggled to stateside buyers, the heroin was then sold to other distributors and high-level dealers, then 'cut' with common substances such as powdered milk or quinine before hitting street level sales. A kilogram of pure heroin could be cut and packaged into ten or more times that amount. The profit margin for drug dealing was astronomical, especially when considering the final product available for users, in the time of Henry Marzette, was around 10% pure. The mob subcontracted the actual 'dealing' of heroin to the African American faction. Black dealers peddled the drug to users who then in turn get hooked and kept coming back for more.

In the late 1960's and early 1970's, estimates regarding the user were around twenty-eight to thirty-five years old, with roughly a $35 a day habit. Added up, it was a lot of money to be made from the top to the bottom of the dope dealing food chain. Detroit was churning out many small time dealers trying to make a quick buck, or simply survive in the difficult economic environment. However, bigger dealers were very protective of their business; locations of drug dens, overall territory and allies. With the drug trade came added dangers like never before seen in organized crime history. Long gone were the days of old "rules of engagement" with law enforcement and innocent civilians.

This is exactly the type of underworld culture that Chester Wheeler Campbell was engulfed in. He was precisely what such an environment required. Campbell's position of enforcement duties parlayed into jobs requiring transportation and distribution of drugs as well. Sometimes, there was collateral damage. Unwitting witnesses, often the drug users themselves, were caught in the crossfire of jobs that took violent turns. The drug dens that seemed to be everywhere in the Pingree, Oakland, and Livernois areas were places where both dealers and addicts were often present at the same time. If a den was raided by rival dealers, or as in some cases - daring thieves out for a free score or cash – addicts getting their fix were simply in the way.

Chester Wheeler Campbell did not discriminate. Addicts, dealers, cops, lawyers, prosecutors, black, white, Italian mobsters or black drug lords; only the money he was receiving mattered. All of the former were equally also potential targets should a contract be offered. He remained closely associated with certain parties over others, but basically Campbell was a well-versed freelancer in the duties of assassination and threats throughout the entire drug underworld. He found it much better to remain largely non-partisan when it came to politics of organized crime.

In 1971 when Chester was fully involved in the heroin-ruled Detroit underworld, President Nixon was declaring a national "war on drugs." On January 28, 1972 – that war was officially signed into law. Nixon called the drug problem, "public enemy number one."

Before the 1970s, policymakers saw drug abuse primarily as a social disease that could be addressed with treatment. After the 1970s, politicians saw drug abuse primarily as a law enforcement problem that could be addressed with aggressive criminal justice policies.

In a piece titled *History of the War on Drugs*, author Tom Head states, "The addition of the Drug Enforcement Administration (DEA) to the federal law enforcement apparatus in 1973 was a significant step in the direction of a criminal justice approach to drug enforcement. If the federal reforms of the Comprehensive Drug Abuse Prevention and Control Act of 1970 represented the formal declaration of the War on Drugs, the Drug Enforcement Administration became its foot soldiers."

War between rival dope dealing factions in the streets of major cities was bad enough for the average citizen to deal with. In the attempt to reduce the problem of drug abuse though, a new dynamic was added when the DEA was created. The government was going after the addicts as much as they were the dealers. And for an already stressed minority community especially, this "war on drugs" was feeling like more of a war on lower income communities and minority members of society.

Going back to the first steps in heroin economics, the farmers made much more money from opium than any other legitimate crops they could grow. However, in no way were those farmers reaping the fortune that others down the line did on a regular basis. The wholesalers who processed the raw opium into heroin were making money. The distributors of the heroin were making money. The street level dealers were making money. In the end, the farmers saw the least amount of rewards for the product, but ultimately the only undeniable losers in the heroin business were the users. Addicted to, imprisoned by, and willing to do anything for a fix of the powdered and liquefied substance. They will steal, cheat, lie, sell things, sell themselves. A universal truth – the user plays a form of Russian roulette with every fix. Besides the insane amount of money spent on fulfilling the addiction, the possibility of overdose and death always linger.

But the illicit drug business exists because there is a demand for the product, and organizations willing to supply that demand. And the money spent does indeed have an impact on economics of legitimate society. Dealers buy things too. People with few lucrative options in mainstream society are employed down the line for everything from street corner dealing to information gathering, delivering to enforcing, and sometimes just for keeping their eyes, ears and mouths shut. They buy things too. Drug money does not sit in vaults. Drug money is spent, even in lawful civilized mainstream society. This is economic reality of drugs.

For drug lords or mobsters to pay large amounts of money, when necessary, to 'remove' an obstacle that inhibits business flow – it has to be worth it and deemed achievable. Chester Wheeler Campbell was viewed as both. Drug money and contract hits had gone hand and hand for many years. Those street tales that speak of Campbell earning upwards of ten-thousand or more on a professional hit, for the time period, may seem outrageous. However, Campbell didn't generally just take out anyone (though a contract was a contract) – he was often hired for special circumstances.

To put the economic rewards in perspective, and if it is to be taken as potentially true, there were concerns for George Bennett during his assault on the drug conspirators. There was genuine worry over a contract that had been placed on his life - $20,000 for his death. A top cop would earn a hit man very high dollar amounts. Because the heroin racket was so very lucrative, spending that kind of cash was viewed as a good investment, if the end result would keep business rolling in the dough.

It's not the pretty flower to blame, but what people can and will do with it thereafter. Chester's Detroit was thriving from it; the rest of Detroit was plagued by it.

CHAPTER EIGHTEEN

THE PEN IS MIGHTIER THAN THE SWORD

"The law isn't justice. It's a very imperfect mechanism. If you press exactly the right buttons and are also lucky, justice may show up in the answer. A mechanism is all the law was ever intended to be."
-Raymond Chandler

THE SUMMER HAD passed with a multitude of ripples running through Detroit's stressed society, the underworld segment included. The mainstream world had endured rioting, rising unemployment, police brutality and corruption. The criminal segment had seen the mob under scrutiny for the Jimmy Hoffa disappearance, the 10th Precinct Conspiracy trials were on the verge of a final ending with some surprising guilty verdicts of drug dealers and dirty cops alike, and Chester Wheeler Campbell spent his time shuffling from county to county, courtroom to courtroom, facing a barrage of legal troubles, with plenty of dramatic antics that made for juicy headlines (when the media wasn't preoccupied with other news).

By October, more feathers were being ruffled. Campbell hadn't forgot about his beef with Orchard Lake's Corporal John Walsh. While the hit man now sat in uncomfortably in the infamous

Jackson Prison, he pondered the search warrant that Walsh was issued back in February. That warrant truly irritated Campbell. Again, Walsh had listed, among the other items, a request to search for suspected PCP, angel dust. But as testimony from the chemist who examined the suspected drugs taken from Campbell's rented Oldsmobile showed – there was no findings of phencyclidine. For Chester, this was perceived as solid grounds to have his case overturned. He considered the use of PCP, by Walsh, on a sworn request for a search warrant, to be perjures at the very least.

Chester still did not consider his own actions as the problem. He really felt the law was out to do him wrong. It's possible he convinced himself of this over time; he considered himself a "victim" for most of his existence. Chester was smart and was capable of understanding the difference between right and wrong. Still, he tried his best to make the Orchard Lake cops look like the lawbreakers.

The more Campbell mulled over the court testimony and warrant particulars, the more it all eventually conjured such immense feelings of disdain towards Corporal Walsh that he felt compelled to share his thoughts with Orchard Lake top brass. As though a straw breaking the camel's back, testimony in court regarding the alleged angel dust found in his possession would stir him to battle back. From Campbell's perspective, fighting the concealed weapons charges was going to be a futile effort, but the confiscated cash (which the tax man had already taken) and charges of PCP possession... these topics made him irate. The Motor City hit man was confident all along there was no angel dust to be found because he didn't have any in the first place.

But again, Corporal John Walsh had specifically made reference to PCP in order to secure a warrant to search Campbell's

Oldsmobile on February 6th. When the crime lab investigator testified in court... well, he basically said there was no conclusive evidence of phencyclidine in the suspected narcotics given to him for testing. Chester Wheeler Campbell hadn't overlooked this bit of courtroom inconsistency and decided to go on the offensive – even though he was caught red handed with all the other items cops suspected he would have.

He began writing letters of all sorts, including motions for new trials and lawsuits against those he viewed as responsible for his incarceration. One of the first such letters was addressed to Orchard Lake's Chief of Police Jack E. Nicholson, bluntly demanding Corporal Walsh be reprimanded for perjury. Heroin and guns were most definitely found in Campbell's possession; the phencyclidine charge was sketchy. Although it was true Corporal John Walsh of Orchard Lake PD listed PCP as one of the reasons for requesting a search warrant on Campbell's rental car trunk, this issue was minor in the eyes of the law. Campbell however saw it as primary reason a search warrant was issued, and thereby in violation of his rights. Now, whether or not Chester actually believed this 'inconsistency' was going to free him is something only he would know. More likely, and as years to come would show, Campbell thoroughly exploited any and every option even remotely available that might get him satisfaction against justice system.

Always the bold one, Campbell had no intention of letting this sleeping dog lie, nor would that be the last of issues he would fight for. He didn't get his way most of the time, but his tenacity and knowledge of the law far exceeded that of any 'typical' criminal, at least in his own mind it did. Chester Wheeler Campbell was smart, cocky and confident.

In the letter dated October 15th, 1975, Campbell typed a request of sorts. One of a thinly veiled attempt at civility, but the end result unmistakably demonstrated pure resentment. This animosity was not only directed towards Corporal John Walsh; he seemed to target law enforcement personnel as a whole.

In accusing Walsh of perjury Chester Wheeler Campbell briefly relates to Orchard Lake's Chief Nicholson how the alleged PCP listed in the original search warrant came under scrutiny during trial. Basically, the chemist's testimony did not verify any of the substances were actually phencyclidine. With that revelation, Campbell felt the search warrant was based on falsified statements made by Corporal Walsh, and therefore he would soon be freed in light of this. It was obvious during previous court proceedings that Chester Campbell and John Walsh were not fond of one another, as they and the attorney's sparred repeatedly. Again, for Campbell – this was business *and* personal. Therefore, in the meantime – he wanted Walsh to pay.

Campbell's former court-appointed attorney Michael Bars says he remembers how adamant his client was about the arresting officer and the prosecuting attorney Michael Izzo. "He did not like John Walsh. He did not like Izzo."

The typed, occasionally misspelled correspondence, to Chief Nicholson reflected how Chester took this 'violation' personally and wanted some reprisal.

He wrote:

"Dear Chief Nicholson:

For your edification and possible action; but, assuredly, for my hereafter action, please be advised of the following.

In seeking a search warrant fro the search of my car, in his affidavit in support thereof, Corporal John Walsh, among other things, swore to having found a substance found by the Michigan State Police Crime

*Laboratory to have been the dangerouse drug: Phencyclidine (PCP);
as, however, the testimony of the chemist showed on the trial, that
statement was perjurious; that it therefore constituted the knowing
use of perjured testimony, not only to obtain my conviction in the
State Court, and, presumably, in an attempt to secure my conviction,
on the same charges, in the Federal Court; which, as a matter of law,
voids them all; it merely being a question of time before the courts rule
in my favor thereon; however, that is another matter, not a subject of
your direct concern or interest.*

*As the commission of perjury is a violation of Federal and State
Law, and a Civil Rights Violation against me, I presume it is an
act "unbecoming a Police Officer" in any police department, however
small?*

*Therefore, on that assumption, this letter is to formally appraise
you thereof, and to seek your disciplinary action against Corporal John
Walsh for his such "unbecoming conduct." The Court's have repeatedly said that there is nothing more dispicable then the commission of
crimes, by law enforcement, in pursuit of criminals, and in the name
of "Law and Order"; and nothing more creates disrespect for law and
law enforcement officers then that; and I agree.*

For your anticipated action in this matter, I am. "

Chester W. Campbell

#91838

P.O. Box E

Jackson, Michigan

Campbell's effort received little feedback, but that did not de-
ter him from moving on to another conflict. He also sought to
fight against the 'habitual criminal' label attached to him. When
Chester's Oakland County case was being "enhanced" by the
prosecutor's use of the Habitual Criminal statute, Michael Bars

was a young attorney, appointed by the court to assist Campbell. "He wanted to rep himself, " Bars says. "He was one hard kind of guy, tough. Stocky, well-built, tight-lipped," he remembered of Campbell's physical and mental demeanor.

Bars felt the court selected him because of his own stature. "I'm a big guy, 6'5' and I think they appointed me to control him."

Bars recalls Chester as a no-nonsense type that could quickly see through any lies and gave more respect to those he knew were also on the level. Once he got to know his client, Bars realized Campbell was only going to cooperate with someone he felt would be truly dedicated to helping his case. After an initial meeting where Chester felt slighted, Bars says they eventually "Gained each other's respect."

Bars was brought into the mix after Oakland County sought to have Campbell's prior record added – assuring a lengthy prison stay. Habitual Criminal. Bars filed a motion in fall of 1977 to "Quash Information and Dismiss Cause." He managed to get a few of the convictions removed on the basis of "unconstitutionality."

In the motion, Bars addressed the original conviction, which was of course for three counts weapons and one-count narcotics. His motion then dissected the prosecution's later attempt to add Campbell's prior record – to bolster a lengthier sentence. Two of the major points were addressed as follows:

7. That on June 23, 1975, after the conviction of the Defendant on the original information, the Prosecutor's Office for the County of Oakland then filed a Supplemental Information, in the Oakland County Circuit Court, alleging Defendant was a Habitual Criminal contrary to M.C.L.A. 769.12 Compiled Laws of 1948.

8. That the Prosecutor's Supplemental Information filed in this cause is defective and constitutionally infirm since said information alleging or charging Defendant with having been a Habitual Criminal was not filed simultaneously with the original information, or at least previous to Defendant's conviction in Kalamazoo County, pursuant to the dictates of People v Stratton, 13 Mich App 350 (1968), and People v Marshall, 41 Mich App 66 (1972).

9. That the aforementioned cases make it mandatory for the Prosecutor to file said Supplemental Information previous to the date of conviction of the defendant charged as a habitual criminal where the Prosecutor has knowledge of the four convictions that the accused person is a prior felon and therefore subject to the Habitual Criminal Act. (See M.C.L.A. 769.13.)

10. That on or about July 11, 1975 your Defendant was sentenced, without objections from the Prosecution on the original information, to 60 months in the State Prison for Southern Michigan. That the Prosecution is therefore estopped from invoking the penal Statute of Habitual Offender provisions because he acquiesced in the trial courts sentencing which was done after the supplemental information was filed but before trial on the issue of Defendant's being a Habitual Offender.

Attorney Bars closed the motion by stating, "The procedure followed by the Prosecutor deprives the Defendant of due process of law, and violates the precepts of fundamental fairness. There is no valid reason for the delay in filing said information and proceeding to trial on said matter and said information must be quashed."

Bars recalls the motion successfully removing a few of the priors, "That saved him time in prison. He would have done life."

He also believes that Chester did in fact have specific targets of anger. "He did not like John Walsh and he did not like prosecutor Mike Izzo." Bars also remembers Chester was particularly incensed by the invasion of his girlfriend Mary Williams' home. "He did not like that either."

It was 1977 before Chester Wheeler Campbell began officially serving time for his crimes in Oakland and Wayne Counties. He was first condemned for his weapons and drug violations stemming from the Orchard Lake incident in February of 1975. Oakland County still used the "habitual criminal" law, based on his prior felonious convictions (the ones remaining after defense attorney Michael Bars had some removed from prosecutor's use), which earned him a twelve year term. Then, he went before a judge to face sentencing based on the guilty verdict for his weapons violations. Besides owning many guns that were illegally modified and stolen, Campbell – as a convicted felon – had broken the law by possessing firearms of any kind. Wayne County hit him with a seven and a half year sentence for that, but not without a fight.

Standing in Judge Robert DeMaschio's U.S. District courtroom, Campbell and his court-appointed attorney refused to make a statement on his behalf. With that, the judge had no choice but to impose the sentence. Campbell chose not to make an official statement, but that didn't mean his mouth was shut. Angry at the whole situation, he verbally clashed with Judge DeMaschio throughout the proceedings. With his trademark toothpick in tow, Campbell faced the judge scowling with visible animosity. During the session, Judge DeMaschio asked the defendant to please remove the toothpick from his mouth. Rather than demonstrate his reputedly cool and business like demeanor, Campbell smugly responded," Why? It doesn't impair my speech any."

Realizing he was destined for another lengthy stay behind bars, yet again, Campbell could not restrain the resent he felt from this hopeless situation. Still, he never blamed his own actions in such situations. To him, it was all bad luck and premeditated conspiracies by law enforcement.

Chester Wheeler Campbell had been quite familiar with the cold and unwelcoming confinement of Jackson Prison. Underworld life was, however, not about to slow down even with Chester off the street. His former associates, clients and enemies were still in a frenzied struggle for heroin dealing supremacy. As for his time behind bars, Campbell would again consume books relating to law, and in turn, penning a series of motions, letters and condemnations. The new decade would come along before Chester would taste freedom again. For the people on his notorious 'hit list' though, knowing Campbell would ever see the light of day from outside a prison cell was an unnerving possibility.

Chester Campbell then, in 1978, began exclusively writing his own motions. He felt confident in representing himself, had been doing legal assistance for years, and certainly knew how the legal system worked – being he'd spent most of his life behind bars. An example of Campbell's handwritten motions, and the manner of which he sought legal relief and his disgust with the prosecution's team of Terrance Boyle and Michael Izzo is illustrated in his 1978 Motion for a New Trial:

8. Because Prosecution witness Terrance Boyle, with the calculated, intentional, prejudicial purpose and effect of prejudicing the jury against Defendant and thus of denying Defendant a fair trial.

9. Because the court refused Defendant's motion for mistrial because of the statements of Terrance Boyle, referred to in Paragraph (8) above.

10. Because the Assistant Prosecuting Attorney, Michael Izzo, collaborated with, aided and induced the high prejudicial testimony of Terrance Boyle, referred to in Paragraph (8) above, and thereby contributed to the denial of a fair trial to the defendant.

11. Because the testimony of Terrance Boyle, referred to in Paragraph (8) above, was inherently incredible as a matter of law, and this should not have contributed to the verdict against the Defendant, where its admission denied the Defendant a fair and impartial trial.

Chester's motion continued to point blame at prosecutors, calling them out for no longer having any witnesses and basically manufacturing evidence against him. He also rallied against the jury being present when his prior records were mentioned, and felt that was sufficient to grant him a new trial as well.

The motion was denied. Chester did not get a new trial, all he gained were more reasons to dislike prosecutors such as Michael Izzo and Terrance Boyle.

CHAPTER NINETEEN

HAROLD, FRANK AND LOTS OF DEAD BODIES

*"The hour of departure has arrived and we go our ways; I to die,
and you to live. Which is better? Only God knows."*
— **Socrates**

IN THE MORNING hours of July 18th, 1979, guests began arriving at a private social gathering establishment on Garfield. The doorman for the Federated Democratic Club was given strict orders to turn away the usual members, as the building was reserved only for a selected few individuals. Business discussions, an underworld meeting, and an ugly reprisal were at hand.

Later, a conversion van sat silent, eerily, unattended and definitely out of place. Police approached the suspicious vehicle, unsure of what they may find inside, but an ominous vibe was certainly in the air. The back doors were then opened, revealing a horrific scene – three lifeless bodies, rigor mortis set in. The scene was quite clear to the police – this was not a typical homicide. These bodies had been here for a little while, but neatly lined in a row. The odor of death is not something easily compared to any other smell. What really struck the police as spine chilling and unusual, from this initial view, it appeared each victim had been mutilated, most likely killed elsewhere and then placed in the vehicle.

Positioned next to one another, each body was paired with a plastic bag nearby. Each brown plastic bag, as police discovered, contained a human head. All three victims, two men and one woman, had been killed by gunshot at another location, and then their bodies further disfigured before being placed in the vehicle. All were decapitated. The hands of both males were also hacked off; one hand from the female removed. The bodies, and amputated parts, were all found together in the back of the van. The van was driven to a spot just a few blocks from a privately owned social club located at 43 Garfield. The area between John R and Erskine, where the vehicle sat parked, was known for drug related issues.

The crime was immediately considered a drug related murder, and investigators were gathering up names as quickly as possible. A homicide, carrying traits such as these, was absolutely intended to send a stark message. There were even a few witnesses to the massacre. A number of people cops wanted to question were very well known individuals in the drug underworld, but the case was not going to be cut and dry by any stretch.

Willie McJoy, Joanne Clark and William Jackson were, as investigators derived from witnesses and evidence at the scene, forced to lie down on the floor in a room of the Federated Democratic Club. Each was then shot in the head and back. Using a meat cleaver, a perpetrator then beheaded each victim. Five of six hands were amputated thereafter by way of the same knife. Why the Clark only had one hand removed was unknown. The headless bodies were loaded into a van and driven just a few blocks away, the vehicle abandoned. Between the multiple gunshot wounds and subsequent mutilations, there was a tremendous amount of bloody evidence. While the bodies were being disposed of, other perpetrators worked feverishly to 'clean' the club up, and dispose of the weapons – a handgun and meat cleaver.

The events of that fateful day were indeed the result of a narcotics territory grievance. McJoy, Clark and Jackson arrived at the club with another man – an East Detroit drug lord with quite a legendary reputation in Detroit. Frank Lee Usher was well known by his intimidating nickname - "Nitti" – an obvious reference to Al Capone's infamous number two man, Frank "The Enforcer" Nitti. Usher and company were greeted by two California hit men, James (Red) Freeman, 35, and Robert (Lefty) Partee, who were called in to settle a dispute with *extreme prejudice*. But what actually transpired that day became yet another of Detroit's bizarre underworld mysteries.

Investigators believed that Adolf "Doc Holliday" Powell, another powerful figure in the drug game and proprietor of a club called La Players Lounge, had wired cash to the men from San Diego. The killers then travelled to Detroit and committed the actual murders inside the Federated Democratic Club. The first arrests did not begin until October, with the apprehension of Usher, who, along with the other suspects, was considered responsible for at least a dozen drug-related murders that occurred over the previous two years.

Then homicide detective Lieutenant Gerald Stewart minced no words, publicly pronouncing the perpetrators as those involved in the previous unsolved murders. "We have 13 or 14 homicides since 1977 that are directly linked in some way to our suspects."

Both Partee and Freeman, the hit men from San Diego, were wanted in connection with a Detroit murder that took place in

January of 1979. Investigators also knew the pair was wanted in New York for weapons charges. Partee and Freeman were not anonymous by any means, even though professional hits have, historically, often been contracted to outsiders. Remaining un-recognizable adds to the element of surprise and limits witnesses and police ability to identify perpetrators. But again, this par-ticular duo had been in police sights for a while. Furthermore, it was their history that helped authorities track down and locate Frank Lee Usher, who had left Detroit to live in Indiana. He was arrested outside Indianapolis and extradited back to Michigan shortly thereafter.

The police were actively hunting down the two men from Cali-fornia, along with another man named Benjamin Fountain, and the suspected mastermind Adolph "Doc Holliday" Powell. Cops had been seeking a sixth person in the murder investigation, forty-three year old Clarence Welton. He was found, dead of a gunshot wound, just a few days before Usher's October 5th arrest.

Police charged Frank Lee Usher with first-degree murder. Witnesses claimed Usher was present in the room where the murders occurred, holding the meat cleaver at one point. Frank Lee Usher and his wife were also subsequently charged with possession of a firearm and ammunition. It was thought he ac-quired such items from his wife, and participated in the shooting stage of the crime. However, when the first three accused were all brought to trial, a juror changed her mind after a guilty verdict was issued. Judge Justin Ravitz, who famously handled much of the 10th Precinct Conspiracy Trial in 1975, first dismissed charges against the handyman/doorman who was accused, then declared a mistrial upon the juror's change of heart.

Partee was later found guilty, but "Doc Holliday" Powell walked out of jail a free man. On the street, he was still considered the mastermind of the whole beheading incident. As Powell exited Wayne County Jail he was questioned by a Detroit Free Press reporter, gleefully replying, "I never want to be in here again. But as long as you believe in God, you're always as free as the rain that falls."

Freeman was acquitted as well. He, however, was soon convicted for unrelated crimes. Frank Usher was tried separately from the other men and found guilty, but appealed quickly. "Nitti" claimed he was originally one of the gunmen's targets, but finagled his way out of being harmed. In return for his life, he had to "assist" the hit men in murder, or the body mutilation and disposal at the very least. The prosecution didn't dispute Usher's "trigger man" denial. They didn't think he actually shot anyone, but were convinced he was part of the overall plot from its inception. He was originally sentenced to life in prison. In the Motor City's long history of organized crime drama, the outcomes for many of these characters would be shaped by more unusual developments, revelations and reprisals. Chester Wheeler Campbell was definitely behind prison walls while such events transpired, having nothing directly to do with them. The business of drug conflict and trade continued with or without his presence. However, the most dangerous enforcer of Detroit was indeed familiar with at least one of the main characters in this seedy tale.

When Frank Lee Usher's name came up in the media, Chester's often did too. Again, Campbell had been in one jail or another most of time since his 1975 arrest in Orchard Lake, but he kept in contact with some associates and had been working steadily up until the point of his arrest. According to some sources, Chester Wheeler Campbell and Frank Lee Usher were known associates. Campbell, being the freelance type, was not a loyalist to any one particular organization. His primary region of business was West Detroit. Usher was considered a kingpin in the East Detroit sector, but also had other business dealing in the western part of town. Campbell, however, allegedly did perform a little work for a ring founded by Harold Morton, at some point in the early 1970's. This is the group where Usher further honed his skills. Frank Lee Usher's name was indeed in one of Campbell's infamous notebooks, simply identified as *"F. Nitti"* with a corresponding telephone number.

"Before he got locked up," says organized crime historian Scott Burnstein, "there was a time for about a year he (Campbell) was basically like on retainer for Usher and Morton."

Harold Morton was one of the many up and coming drug dealers looking to fill in the gaps opened when Henry Marzette died in 1972. The worst of the drug territory wars, that gripped the city during Marzette's polarizing effort to gain independence from the mafia, were basically over. There was no cease-fire type of ending, but rather a brief decline in the overly brazen types of killings that had been occurring frequently during those couple of years. When a power vacuum develops, especially in gangland history, another level of conflict begins. New groups and individuals were definitely looking for a piece of the pie. The Harold Morton Organization, as it was known both on the streets and by law enforcement, had its very own intimidating enforcer – Frank Lee Usher officially filled that role. Because Big Frank Nitti could instill similar fear as Chester Wheeler Campbell (and they were known associates) – police, media and underworld types often discussed both characters in the same street lore conversations. After the 1979 beheading case, Usher's name was immediately synonymous with the unfathomable underworld viciousness that Chester Campbell was known for. They were, respectively, two of the most notorious men Detroit had seen since they era of the violent Purple Gang.

As Scott Burnstein had said, again, it wasn't a long period of collusion, but Campbell certainly did have some dealings with Morton's group, especially Frank Lee Usher who was also a well-known tough guy.

Usher was by no means a new kid on the drug trafficking circuit; he had a criminal record dating back before the time Campbell was arrested in Orchard Lake. Adding to the mystery of all these characters, a judge had, in 1975, expunged Frank Lee Usher's criminal record. Nobody seemed to know why this action was taken. The judge responsible, Dalton Robertson, erased not one, but three offenses from Usher's criminal history on August 15, 1975 – right smack in the heart of Detroit's most tumultuous summer of organized crime history. One of those was an armed robbery attempt, which under Michigan law, is a capital offense thus making it ineligible for such action. Further, according to that law, only one offense can be expunged from a criminal record – not multiple offenses.

The judge, who was questioned years later about the incident, simply told the press, "I guess a lawyer must have brought the motion before me." Interestingly, Usher's attorney at that time, Evelyn Cooper, later went on to become a judge herself, in the same court as Robertson.

The twists and turns of Detroit's criminal underbelly had essentially been more the rule than the exception, dating back at least to the time of bootleggers. Long before Chester Wheeler Campbell became a prominent player in the underworld of Detroit, the dramatic feuding of rival drug lords, and the unusual manners in which some operated without interruption, was astounding.

Usher worked his way through the violent drug trafficking element, earning his criminal stripes while working in Morton's organization. Harold Morton's method of smuggling was often a *hands-on* approach. He regularly employed the use of "mules" – people who actually carry the contraband on or in the bodies. Women, his wife included, were physically smuggling various quantities of heroin via air and automobile travel methods.

Morton's fall from power began in November 1977. First, he and two female companions – Sandra Jones and Gloria Roe – embarked on a trip to Amsterdam. The trek was arranged to secure narcotics. After spending several days there, Morton showed the women packages he wanted them to securely and discreetly carry back to the States. He directed each of them to hide a package down their pants, tightly against the crotch, which they did, and then move about the room so he could judge if anything was visible. Once he felt the packages were well hidden on the Roe and Jones's bodies, the trio headed to the airport for the trip back to New York.

On November 18th, Gloria Roe and Sandra Jones were detained in JFK airport's customs. A subsequent search revealed the hidden packages – 29% pure heroin, half pound each. Morton, who had entered a different customs line, was also detained but he wasn't carrying any contraband. The women, however, quickly told the investigating DEA Agents that Morton was behind the smuggling scheme. All three were taken into custody and transported to jail in the city.

Morton was able to get out on a bail using property he had in Detroit as collateral. The women however remained in New York. S. Allan Early, the same attorney that helped Chester Campbell plea down his murder conviction in 1969, took care of having Roe and Jones released as well, just a couple weeks after Morton.

Harold Morton was nervous. The possibility that anyone may take the witness stand against him was looming and he needed to find out if Roe or Jones were talking to prosecutors.

In early December, Morton met with both Roe and Jones in the offices of attorney S. Allan Early. He asked them both point-blank if they were willing to "do time" for him. Roe conceded on the condition that Morton would take care of her family while she served. Jones was not willing to do hard time and told Morton as much. Gloria Roe left the meeting, but Morton and Jones continued their discussion, which presumably involved a plea and or warning to Jones to change her mind.

Jones left in a distraught state, quickly making plans to visit family in the South. She was visibly frightened and told Roe she feared for her life. Sandra Jones visited Alabama and then made a trip to Southern California. She wanted to stay as far away from Detroit and Harold Morton as humanly possibly.

Morton decided to hire a Detroit cab driver, Thornell McKnight, to eliminate Jones (who he referred to as Miss S.). The price for the hi was only$2500. Jones lived with her young daughter in San Diego, but McKnight tracked her down in Los Angeles visiting her brother. On December 11, 1977, Thornell McKnight forcibly took Jones from the brother's home and dragged her into a dark alley. He then put two slugs from a .38 caliber into Sandra Jones chest, killing her instantly.

It did not take long for Los Angeles investigators to figure out McKnight's relation to the murder, and that led quickly back to Harold Morton. McKnight knew he was in deep trouble, so he agreed to testify and further implicated Morton's wife, twenty-five year old Hilda Singleton, as being a willing and present player in the murder plot. The law gave McKnight a second-degree murder conviction. Hilda Singleton got ten years for her role. Morton, well, he was getting the full power and fury of justice thrown at him. On April 11, 1978, he was found guilty of violating the civil rights of Sandra Jones. It took over a year for sentencing, but on Tuesday April 29th, 1980, thirty-two year old Harold Morton was escorted into U. S. District Court to hear his fate. Judge Robert Takasugi then sentenced Morton to life in prison for hiring Thornell McKnight to murder Sandra Jones.

Usher rose to prominence after Morton's fall in 1977. "Nitti" was no longer the number two guy; he was the de facto boss and took to the position with authoritative demeanor. He already carried a reputation of fearsome proportions and was considered well connected to mob factions on top of that. East Detroit was Usher's kingdom, though he was respectably prominent in the West as well. Most monarchs in the drug underworld are eventually challenged, sometimes toppled, and as such, Frank Usher had plenty of enemies, just as every other drug lord before him had to contend with.

"Usher's group was really the last holdout that was still working with the Italians," Scott Burnstein explains. "Tony Giacalone was sort of a mentor to Usher."

Frank Lee Usher's organization was known as *Murder Row*. There was however a powerful group in opposition to Murder Row, and basically every other established drug-dealing organization. "The other group," adds Burnstein, "the one that wanted total independence was Y.B.I."

Still, Usher continued to create a name for himself, becoming a bigger and bigger fish in the dope dealing pond. This rise in status and power invited deceit and murderous plots. Whatever really transpired at the Federated Democratic Club that fateful day in 1979 may never be known. Some theorized that Usher was actually planning to eliminate Adolf "Doc Holliday" Powell. The whole event was certainly filled with conspiracy, but who was out to get whom was a mystery. Doc Holliday had walked free and clear; Usher was appealing his conviction. More insidious plots were hatching and the story was far from over. Doc Holliday was still going to face the music for his alleged role in the Democratic Club murder conspiracy.

CHAPTER TWENTY

BLACK ORCHIDS

"I say a murder is abstract. You pull the trigger and after that you do not understand anything that happens."
- Jean-Paul Sartre

John "Johnny Coach" Cociu was a father, husband, and co-owner of two Detroit lounges – *The Black Orchid* and the *Black Orchid West*. His business partner in both bars was none other than Frank Lee Usher. Although being in business with Usher was sure to draw unwanted attention from the law, the fifty-seven year old Cociu had also been, by January 1980, under surveillance for at least a few months for, as police put it, "having his hands in a lot of pies." Cociu was thought to be involved in other non-legitimate business dealing, not exclusively 'drug related.' Police were well aware of his association with Usher, and other questionable characters, some with mob ties.

"Johnny Coach" Cociu left the Black Orchid West, located on Livernois, after calling his wife to say he'd be home soon. That was at 5:00 pm. His home in Lakeville, Oakland County was a thirty-five mile trip north from the lounge in West Detroit.

Concerned after the hours had passed and Cociu hadn't come home yet, his wife called the Black Orchid and spoke to some of her husband's hired help. Twenty-four hours later, employees of the Black Orchid West found a spare set of keys to Cociu's car, a 1978 Cadillac, which was still parked in the bar's lot. They looked the car over, but no sign of Cociu. They opened the trunk, however, to a most horrifying sight. Police quickly made their way to the scene.

Investigators determined unknown assailants had shot to John Cociu to death, and then beheaded him. His killers used the car keys Cociu had in his pocket to open the trunk of the Cadillac, where they stashed the headless body. Investigators removed Cociu's nude body from the trunk. The head was nowhere to be found.

He had been shot in his side and most likely died of that wound before his murderer's decapitated him. Some of the investigating detectives weren't so sure the murder was positively a drug related crime. While that scenario was plausible - a retaliatory punishment for the Democratic Club incident his business partner Frank Lee Usher was jailed in relation to - organized crime investigators considered other possibilities. They were not speaking to details or specifics; giving the curious press very little information as to exactly 'what' Cociu was involved in. What did become clear – John Cociu was also a business agent for the local 575 Riggers and Machinery Erector's Union. That office happened to be located in the same building as the Black Orchid West where his body was found. The implication was Cociu had some underworld dealing beyond the drug trade with Usher, probably mob related. Investigators told the press they actually perceived the murder and beheading as "staged" to look like a drug related assassination, most likely planned as such simply to throw cops off course. If it was related to the drug underworld, they figured the killing could have been a result of the "turmoil" during a vacuum of power in leadership, since Usher had been locked up back in October of the previous year. Still, "Johnny Coach" was considered a man with mafia associations and cops remained tight-lipped as to the dead man's alleged, and numerous underworld dealings.

One official told the press it would be unusual if Cociu were under surveillance because, "he's too well insulated," from his suspected hidden business dealings in the underworld. While some investigators were outright denying any suspicions or prior surveillance on Cociu, others were willing to offer insight to the contrary. It was reported that "other" police agencies had indeed kept tabs on Cociu and he was seen with known criminal fixtures who were also being observed. "Johnny Coach" was suspected of being in cahoots with thieves just a few years earlier – particularly for the "Wrecking Crew" organization of burglars who's reign of terror in affluent neighborhoods came to an end in 1977 with numerous arrests. The group, ski mask wearing bandits that usually bound and gagged homeowners, were sometimes considered "nice" people (one time stopping to feed a hungry toddler before leaving a robbed residence). Cociu had been under investigation for 'fencing' the Wrecking Crew's bounty of stolen goods.

More recent to the time of his death, he was also thought to have business interests in two hotels in Detroit's Cass Corridor – a known haven for prostitution, drugs and murder. The region was a highly treacherous place for civilians and criminals alike. Drug dealers, serial killers, hookers (and their often-violent clients), and the average civilian intermingled in this place, one of the most downtrodden and dangerous of areas (from the mid 1970's through mid 1980's a number of prostitutes were brutally murdered in the area, many unsolved). Police observations of the entire zone were common, therefore when known or suspected figures in illicit dealings were seen there... cops kept tabs. If Cociu did indeed have hidden interests there, cops were sure it was principally involvement in a prostitution ring. Regardless of what "Johnny Coach" did or did not have his hands in, the fact was his murder was particularly brutal and very reminiscent of the murder scene less than a year before that his business partner Frank Lee "Nitti" Usher was charged for. Furthermore, investigators and the press had information that profits from both *The Black Orchid* establishments were providing at least some, if not all, of the cash needed for Usher's legal defense bills. But for every side of a story there is an alternative. "Johnny Coach" was well liked by his employees. He was considered a low-key gentleman who was very generous to anyone in need. "Happy go lucky," one employee said of his personality. His employees weren't the only ones saying nice things about Cociu; other sources told the press and police that he was a likeable guy who never drank alcohol and kept reserved in his business endeavors.

John Cociu's story had ended, but Frank Lee Usher's was ongoing. His would take more unusual turns over the next several years. So too was Chester Wheeler Campbell's. While Detroit was reeling over the horrific crimes of the past year (very reminiscent of, but even more gruesome than the two year dope wars of the early 1970's), and Usher was facing a life behind bars, Campbell was expecting to make a grand return to the city. Around the same time Cociu's murder made local news headlines, Campbell was receiving what he thought would be the best information of his life – parole.

CHAPTER TWENTY ONE

WHILE CHESTER S AWAY, THE GANGSTERS WILL PLAY

"One of the many lessons that one learns in prison is, that things are what they are and will be what they will be."
- Oscar Wilde

CHESTER WHEELER CAMPBELL was, by prison accounts, a rather good boy while serving in Jackson's infamous facility. He accumulated "good behavior" credits, and extra credit. Regardless of whether or not the habitual criminal was merely working the system for what he foresaw as a fast-track exit from incarceration, or realizing that behaving in prison was probably much easier on his aging body than facing the harsh repercussions of being a troublemaker – Campbell served his sentence without incident. He spent most of his days pondering, planning, and fashioning his own motions to the court system.

Acting on his own behalf, Campbell filed reams, literally, page upon page of legal maneuvers in the pursuit of his own idea of justice. By 1981, Chester Wheeler Campbell had already tied up the legal system with a multitude of lawsuits. In one such suit – Campbell vs. Ralph B. Guy., et al. - the United States District Court made note of Campbell's incessant and seemingly regularly filed suits noting, " This plaintiff has filed nineteen lawsuits with this Court since 1960. Fourteen of which have been initiated since 1975."

Of the cases the court pointed out, two were lawsuits against Orchard Lake Corporal John Walsh, one against Judge Ingraham and another against Judge Alice Gilbert, all dating back to the mid and later 1970's. The latter two were drawn up by Chester himself and claimed both Gilbert and Ingraham had violated his civil rights. Judge Gilbert remembers that case didn't go very far, and was even able to find some humor in the whole situation.

"I do remember at one point pleadings were served upon me in Federal Court, that Campbell brought against me for violation of Civil Rights," she recalls. "So was Judge Ingraham for making his bond too high. Campbell was representing himself. I wasn't too worried about it because I was in performance of a judicial role. The matter was dropped. But what impressed me was the pleadings were quite professionally drawn and I assumed, incorrectly, that some attorney had drawn it up. He was asking for damages. He asked for more damages from me than my colleague, and I was the one who set the lower bond. So I said to everyone who was around, 'Campbell knows I'm more collectable than my colleagues.'"

Campbell went on the offensive and fought for everything from the return of confiscated cash and civil rights violations to launching vengeful lawsuits against cops, prosecutors, even newspaper and television reporters for perjury and other perceived crimes. At times, he hired professional legal assistance. For the most part though, following the 1977 leg of incarceration, Campbell stood as his own counsel, drawing up legal motions from his cell and sending them off in the mail. As Judge Gilbert and others had said, Campbell was rather impressive in his legal knowledge. Most of his money had been confiscated and spent on legal fees over the years, so the determination to do things on his own was also out of necessity. Some of his attempts were quite admirable, almost reasonable. Most, however, morphed from loosely-based questions of fact to purely agitated rants – Hail Mary throws in hopes of a win in final seconds.

Campbell had a very legitimate cause of concern in the first month of 1980 when those 'good credits' won him an early release, or so he thought. In January of the new decade, Chester was informed the "good time" and "special good time" credits he rightfully earned while serving his sentence had put him good graces with the parole board. Yes, Campbell was set to go free from the confines of Southern Michigan Prison after serving hard time for drug and firearms violations, and being a habitual criminal. However, there were plenty of people who did not want the paid assassin returning to the free world anytime soon.

Campbell expected, from what he was informed on January 22, that he would be eligible for parole in just a couple weeks. What he didn't know – the Oakland County Prosecutor's Office was also aware of his pending release and was actively working to halt the parole. The weapon wielded by the office? A statute, M.C.L.A. Sec. 769.12(3). In part, it states that habitual criminals – which Chester Wheeler Campbell was officially labeled – may not be paroled "before the minimum fixed by the sentencing judge."

The prosecutor's office conferred with prison officials and the State Attorney General. All came to the agreement that parole should not be available to a habitual criminal. Campbell's parole opportunity was revoked, the day before he was to go free, on orders of Attorney General Frank J. Kelley, and he was furious. He went on to fashion his own legal motions to the courts in an attempt to gain release, along with a little retribution. His efforts were mostly in vain though. His primary argument was based on a belief that parties, including the Attorney General, prison officials and Oakland County Prosecutors - L. Brooks Patterson - specifically, had "conspired to deprive him his right to parole." The statute used by Oakland County prosecutors was formidable, so Chester Campbell ended up serving another few years in prison. Habitual offenders, under the Michigan law, cannot use "good time" credits to reduce a sentence. He never ceased filing motions and appeals though.

Even L. Brooks Patterson, the Oakland County prosecutor who appeared on Campbell's alleged 'hit list' in 1975 was somewhat stunned by tenacity and ability behind the reams of legal motions filed with his office. He said of Chester's talents, "He's not stupid. He's not some dumb street person." His office was frequently sent copies of the handwritten legal motions. "Three reams, and I'm not kidding, of legal documents," Patterson told the press. "At least two of which, if my memory serves me, went as far as the Supreme Court."

Chester absolutely did get some of his motions far up the judicial ladder, but he was usually denied, at some point along the way, in his requests for overturning convictions, monetary returns, and motions to suppress evidence. It did not stop him from continually learning and executing new ways to twist the law for his own redemption. He fancied himself quite the amateur lawyer, if not a better one altogether than those he faced continually from the prosecution.

One of the many new organizations to mar the streets of Detroit, while Chester was in prison, with drug trafficking was undeniably the Young Boys Inc. They forged a very lucrative heroin business from street corner dealing in the late 1970's. By 1982, the organization was a force to be reckoned with. Although they would become more infamous in the mid to late 1980's, once the crack epidemic was in full force, Y.B.I. was making headlines much earlier.

Bernard "Shango" Stroble was a Detroit native, reformed felon, and trying to clean up the neighborhood where his mother lived. Stroble had an infamous reputation – he was credited as the leader of a convict uprising at Attica in 1971. But Shango had reportedly been determined to battle the narcotics problem since his return to civilian life. He was tired of dope dens and pushers basically running the neighborhood and was known to take a physical stance if necessary to make his point.

In the winter of 1982, Shango reached his limit and beat up on three junkies or dealers that frequented an apartment above his shoe repair shop. Some of Stroble's friends said unknown occupants of high-end luxury cars, Mercedes and Cadillac's, then drove around the scene yelling threats of revenge. Shango was not known for being easily intimidated and the beating was intended to send a message – dope dealing not welcome here. His mother, who was a pastor and restaurant proprietor, said her son was known as 'tough' on the streets and was angry with dealers using the restaurant as a new hangout.

The associates of the three beating victims were determined to exact revenge; the verbal threats were not just braggadocio.

Two day following the incident, Bernard "Shango" Stroble drove to his mother's house. As soon as he parked the car in her driveway, the blast of a shotgun took his life. Only hours after Shango was killed by the execution-style shot o his head, his store was burglarized and the pushers 'reopened' the drug den in the apartment above. Some media and law enforcement fingers had pointed directly at the Young Boys Inc. organization.

Also transpiring in the latter months of 1982, Frank Lee "Nitti" Usher was granted an appeal on his first-degree murder conviction. His argument was two-fold; he did not believe the evidence supported his role as a murderer in the first-degree, and, he was not in possession of a firearm. The court found the evidence against him was sufficient for a first-degree murder charge. Usher and his attorney Steve Fishman were not going to give up. More strange events were going to unfold soon.

For the time being though, now resonating with power throughout Detroit were the new generation of dealers, including groups such as Y.B.I. (Young Boys, Inc.) and the Davis Family, among others. Even the scope of importation had changed during the time Campbell was in Jackson Prison.

Also while Chester was still serving time in 1982, Detroit officials also took notice of yet another type of heroin flooding the streets. "Iranian White" was the name bureaucrats had identified it by, and the traffickers weren't black kingpins or white mobsters. This was coming from Middle Eastern traffickers, many of whom thought to be from the Dearborn area.

Mexican brown heroin was common in Detroit during the 1970's and the Asian *white* version, the highly prized more pure product, was available also. This Iranian variety was, however, causing more distress for DEA because the United States' relationship with Iran had, of course, been basically obliterated after the 1979 overthrow of the Shah and hostage crisis.

The DEA agent in charge at the time, Joseph Salvemini, told the press how native Arab-Americans in Dearborn and Western Wayne County were importing Iranian White. He stated the agency's belief that, "The amount of Iranian heroin entering the country has been increasing since the Shah fled the country in 1979."

How much heroin was pouring into Detroit from all sources combined? The government estimated the dollar amount in the hundreds of millions. The Motor City was considered the number 2 center of heroin traffic in the entire nation. New York was number one.

The U.S. Attorney for the Eastern District of Michigan had publicly warned of just how close to the number one spot Detroit was, having said, "When you consider the difference in populations between the two cities, we're virtually certain that heroin sales in Detroit far outstrip those in New York on a per capita basis."

The increase in dope traffic through Detroit between 1981 and 1982 even provoked President Ronald Reagan's action. Both the President and First Lady were adamant in waging war against the increasing drug problem the United States was facing.

In the fall of 1982, the President formally named Detroit as one of twelve "bases" for a new interagency task force that was implemented to "crack down" on the expansive and lucrative drug trade. To bankroll Reagan's war on drugs required astounding amounts of cash. With the implementation of the special task force, the government was looking at 1600 new agents being added, and a price tag estimated between $160 and $200 million dollars.

Turkish heroin was also making its way into Detroit, being trafficked through the old school "French Connection" method. In that manner, the raw opium would be shipped to Italy and Corsica, and then sent off to Marseilles for the final processing step. The connection itself was no longer anywhere near the impact levels of a decade prior. After Turkey conceded to ban opium in the early 1970's, and international arrests dismantled the organization of crime lords behind it, the French Connection was never the same. Still, Turkish heroin was available. Investigators believed the wholesale shipments would arrive on the East Coast or Gulf Coast, then smuggled via car or plane into Michigan. At the time, officials didn't believe much of the narcotics were smuggled through Canada, because agents were allegedly watching the border closely.

The Iranian heroin was something altogether new and they weren't sure how it got into the hands of importers living in Michigan. They were aware, however, that the Iranian variation was much more potent than the Mexican heroin, and cost around $13 a dose at the time. Officials were definitely pointing fingers, convinced it was from the Persian population of Dearborn. Although there were Persians in Dearborn, the area's population was much more consistent with a majority of Chaldean, Lebanese, Iraqi and European descendants. Little more was every publicly mentioned regarding the so-called "Iranian White" connection.

The Motor City was apparently being bombarded with dope from every direction and by a multitude of organizations. The drug dilemma was going to cause more blood to spill. Some of the retribution dated back to the 1979 Federated Democratic Club murders. Doc Holliday Powell had been running his own racket successfully since his 1980 acquittal in the case. However, there were those that sought to teach him a lesson. It was 1983.

In the early afternoon hours of Saturday, January 22, four men entered the La Players Lounge in Northwest Detroit. Two men took position by a bank of pay phones. The other pair of the men were greeted by owner Adolf "Doc Holliday" Powell at the bar. The welcoming proprietor had three glasses of Cognac lined up, pulled out a crisp fifty-dollar bill, and felt the split-second pain of shrapnel entering his body.

Powell had been hit at close range by a shotgun blast. The assailant then turned and fired on a customer trying to escape. Another blast struck a twenty-three year old barmaid – first day on the job. The customer escaped with his life; the barmaid died at the scene, along with Doc Holliday.

Two of the four alleged perpetrators were captured, one a prison escapee. Witnesses claimed Gregory Barnett took credit for the shot that killed both Holliday and the waitress. "Did you see that motherfucker when he got hit?" Barnett allegedly bragged, "When you snitch, things like this happen to you."

But in sync with all the bizarre outcomes of so many legal dramas in Detroit... both men were eventually acquitted in the murders. Nobody was ever convicted for the murder of Adolf "Doc Holliday" Powell and his employee Jeannette Askew.

What would all of this meant to someone like Chester Wheeler Campbell? Most likely, it didn't matter any more than the possibility of supplementary business opportunities for his line of work, or worst case scenario – ripples in whatever gig was going on at the moment. In October of 1983, he was preoccupied in his cell still trying to get back the money confiscated from his home in February of 1975. The United States Court of Appeals, Sixth Circuit, went over the case Chester Wheeler Campbell v. Joseph

Shearer, to determine if the plaintiff was deprived of property - specifically $280,100.

The court argued the case while Campbell sat in prison, still feeling the sting of his parole being revoked in 1980. He hoped this particular motion would get him some monetary relief. After all, this was the single case in Campbell's long history of legal motions whereby the courts actually ruled in his favor. A decade had passed since the IRS and Treasury Departments snatched up Chester's horde of cash. The courts agreed that police had no right to take the money in the search of his home in February 1975, but the bitter pill Campbell had to swallow was that once the tax man got the money – there was virtually no way to every get it back. On the bright side, he was going to see daylight from outside prison walls soon.

In September of 1984, he finally left the confines of Jackson Prison. Campbell was set free and promptly returned to his home on Ivanhoe in West Detroit. His legal plight over the last decade had depleted most of his money, but he still owned the house. Even though he technically won his old battle for the return of $280,000 dollars taken from his home in 1975, that money never made it back to him, and he was going to need some income. West Detroit was still rife with organized crime – the only thing Campbell had intimate knowledge and knowhow of.

What's a former freelance assassin to do? Here was a black man, fresh out of prison, in his early fifties, who's only legitimate job title ever held was that of a driver for a funeral parlor. Detroit was still a racially divided city, and having the words "convicted felon" on record is not something most employers actively look for in potential job candidates.

So Chester did what Chester knew best – reenter the heroin-based underworld enforcement business. Even though he'd been away for a while, Campbell never felt he lost that edge, that cunning, that skill of manipulation and fear. Furthermore, he still had a few proprietary interests to bolster his bank account, and clean that 'extra' cash he was ready to start earning again.

The scope of narcotics traffic had changed over time. There were new players in the game, and improved methods. Campbell was good at his chosen profession, but he was aging, not to mention most of his old comrades in crime were either dead or in jail themselves. It was the early 1980's and cocaine was still gaining popularity as the high-priced luxury drug. An up-and-coming, ultra addictive and deadly "cheap alternative" to pricey powder cocaine – which would come to be known universally as "crack" - was on the horizon. Still, heroin was a staple in the city and always had a good share of the illicit drug consuming market. Perhaps against the odds, but Chester Wheeler Campbell was able to re-establish himself as a proficient and reliable enforcement entity within the Motor City's underworld culture.

A turf war in the drug trade was one of the many ways a man like Campbell could earn a living, keeping busily employed. He still wanted to live and operate like a gangster, plenty of money in tow. So whatever the drug scourged city underworld could offer as a business opportunity, which was fine, so long as the cash was steadily rolling in. Chester was suited for the roles of courier, dealer, enforcer, spy, assassin… whatever needed done, he felt confident and capable. Perhaps against the odds, but Chester Wheeler Campbell was able to re-establish himself as a proficient and reliable enforcement entity within the Motor City's underworld culture.

He wasn't without detractors though. New blood ran through kingpin hierarchy, and a few old foes hadn't forgotten equally long-standing grudges with the hit man. Long gone were the days of the old ruling class. Though legends on the street, drug lords such as Henry Marzette, Harold Morton and Frank Usher were no longer on the proverbial and active kingpin marquee. Virtually anyone who was a high roller in the drug game of the 1970's was dead or in prison. Only a very select few were still making their presence known.

CHAPTER TWENTY TWO

NEW BLOOD REIGNS, OLD BLOOD STAINS

"I'm not interested in preserving the status quo; I want to overthrow It."

-Niccolo Machiavelli

REGARDLESS OF WHERE the dope was coming from, the local chieftains always needed the services of men like Chester Wheeler Campbell. He went about his business, a little distribution here, some intimidation there, and religiously stashing money in every corner of his home, car and clothing. There was a side to his personality that virtually invited unseen dangers though. Besides being very systematic and recognizable, Campbell jaunted around town with an air of immortality. Again, his confidence was unabashed.

Chester left his home early in the day on April 14 1985, heading for an auto repair joint on Oakland. He frequented this establishment, as he did so many others in the area, for business and everyday regular needs. He still had proprietary and investment interests in a few businesses, Wheeler's Total Service certainly one of them. On this particular day however, Chester's somewhat routine movements were going to put him in grave danger. As a professional assassin, a gangster, and an all-around fearsome sort of character – there will always be those patiently waiting for some reprisal. Although he was arguably the best-experienced and skilled spy in the underworld... he was not the only one keeping an eye on important targets. This was not a typical day for Chester Wheeler Campbell. The tables were turning, and he was the mark.

He pulled his car into the bay, left it to the mechanic while he waited. Chester then grabbed himself a seat and proceeded to read the days headlines. As he sat and perused the newspaper, a vehicle suspiciously approached the Oakland Street address. Once the car rolled up on the repair shop, the occupants spotted Campbell in clear view. Chester looked up only to see the glimmer of gunmetal pointed in his direction.

Before he could make an escape from this potentially life-threatening situation, a barrage of bullets sprayed into the repair shop. Many of the rounds pierced the establishment's wall, but four of those projectiles struck Campbell. His head was grazed by one bullet; his legs struck three times. The would-be assassins made a quick escape while Campbell lay bleeding. He had no time to dodge the attack; he did not have quick access to weapons. Chester was a sitting duck this time.

Seriously wounded, he was taken to the hospital in critical condition. Campbell had lost a significant amount of blood and would endure a lengthy stay, complete with major surgery and an even longer healing time thereafter.

Oddly, the incident barely made the news. It wasn't until Campbell came out of an eleven-hour surgery, a month later, which reporters tried to get a statement from him. Chester Wheeler Campbell, the consummate hoodlum, was not about to squeal on his attackers, regardless of the circumstances. He wouldn't say if he even knew who the assailants were or why he was possibly a target. That was not his style. Campbell believed in retribution by his own methods. He did offer the press one characteristically unforthcoming comment, "I've got nothing newsworthy to say."

Someone wanted Campbell dead, but they obviously weren't as adept in their duty as the intended target had been for decades. Their failure merely demonstrated how resilient Chester Wheeler Campbell really was. Moreover, the fact that he survived made his own ego-driven perception all the more skewed. Chester was actually proving himself right; he was almost untouchable.

After several months of recovery, Campbell was gearing up for more outlaw activity. For him, business was business and even as he approached his mid-fifties – there was no slowing Campbell down.

Chester's old associate Frank Lee Usher wasn't ready to call it quits either. Now forty years old, he was still fighting to get his first-degree murder conviction overturned, and he was making some headway. In September, Usher conviction was set-aside in Recorder's Court. Judge David Kerwin granted "Nitti" a new trial, but Wayne County prosecutors were flabbergasted and upset at the ruling, going so far as calling the Judge's decision, "Illogical."

Usher was ecstatic, looking out over the people in the courtroom – he smiled and threw up a high five in the air.

The prosecutors knew that even though five years had passed since Usher was originally convicted, there was a chance he could actually get a brand new trial. Judge Kerwin's logic for the move on Usher's behalf was based on issues that erupted during the 1980 trial. One of the star witnesses, a woman named Cynthia Skeens, claimed Usher spoke to her about "taking out" witnesses from the original murder incident. But Skeens' statements came seven days into trial as a 'surprise' and the Assistant Prosecutor said he had forgotten about the statements until then. The judge wanted to bar Cynthia Skeens' comment, but The Supreme Court decided her testimony did not require advance warning.

Skeens, who in 1981 was kept in protective custody at police headquarters during her testimony against Usher, was the subject of further controversy herself. During her stay in the jail, she joined a fellow prisoner – Gayle York – in a sex scandal, where the two would be allowed to drink alcohol, roam freely and even be taken to restaurants and hotels, by guards, in return for sexual favors.

When push came to shove on the legality of the issues at hand, Frank Usher was indeed going to be granted a retrial, much to the dismay of prosecutors. It would take a few more years, but his day in court was inevitable.

In December of 1986, another subject of the Federated Democratic Club murders – Denise McGilmer- had made headlines. She was found dead in a park, gunshot wound to the head. McGilmer had served time after investigators found her identification inside the van where the three beheaded bodies were dumped. After she was arrested, Judge Justin Ravitz offered her immunity in return for testimony. She declined the offer, though admitted she feared for her life. McGilmer remained in the Detroit area though, and never did testify against anyone involved in the case. Her own family publicly said they didn't believe her death was in relation to the 1979 incident, and police felt compelled to offer no comment either way. Whatever the circumstances surrounding McGilmer's murder, the fact remained... very few people who were involved in the original beheading incident were still alive. Those that were alive, well, most were in jail.

CHAPTER TWENTY THREE

DEJA VU

"No punishment has ever possessed enough power of deterrence to prevent the commission of crimes. On the contrary, whatever the punishment, once a specific crime has appeared for the first time, its reappearance is more likely than its initial emergence could ever have been."

- **Hannah Arendt**

FROM HIS RETURN to the seedy side of streets in Detroit he knew so well, Chester had seen, done and endured enough to further convince his ego that he was basically unstoppable. He finally saw freedom even after his adversary – Oakland County Prosecutor's Office at the forefront – fought hard to prevent him from being able to step foot outside the confines of Jackson Prison. Upon reentering society, Campbell moved back into his home on Ivanhoe, bought a couple cars and swiftly reconnected with his pre-prison lifestyle. Chester Wheeler Campbell was back to work, providing his enforcement skills wherever a paying client required. He even survived an attempt on his life, though it left him with at least four more permanent scars. He was tenacious and avaricious; money was to be made and he had no intentions of missing an opportunity to acquire it.

He had been keeping busy in the Motor City upon parole in September of 1984 well through 1987: his services always in demand. Although cocaine was the big deal since the disco era, and 'crack' cocaine began infiltrating cities like no monster before it, Chester was still a major player in the always-lucrative age-old heroin trade. If he had any dealing in the crack game at all – it was miniscule. In fact, with all the dope Campbell ever had in his possession, and the dealers with whom he worked, heroin remained the prominent theme throughout. His business dabbled in cocaine, but by and large he didn't stray too much from the business of 'smack' and the less lucrative but always popular – marijuana. Crack cocaine was not only an entirely unique beast of a drug, but it's sale on the streets was being done by anyone and everyone who wanted a quick buck and willing to work a corner. The new generation of dope peddlers were younger, their product more powerful, and until a few prominent figures organized it – dealing was a free for all. At its very core, crack produced a very different type of business system than what old schoolers like Campbell were used to.

By this time it didn't matter to cops what drugs Chester handled, or which dealers he did or didn't freelance for, nearly as much as the entirety of the whole scenario comprised of such smaller parts did. The police and prosecutors were literally at wit's end with the reputed assassin still roaming freely, doing whatever dirty deeds, and always expanding the larger picture of Detroit's crime problems. The time had come to remove Chester Wheeler Campbell from free society, once and for all.

The law never actually put him away for being a 'hit man' and they couldn't prove beyond a shadow of a doubt that he murdered, or arranged the murders of Roy Parsons, James Lee Newton (Watusi Slim) and the handful of other unsolved victims listed in his notebooks dating back to 1975. They even had to drop the case against him and his associate Leroy "Bang Bang" James for the attempted murder of Wiley Reed during the 10th Precinct Conspiracy investigation. His 1977 conviction for concealed weapons and drug violations (The 1975 Orchard Lake arrest) really only led to incarceration for a short time – a twelve-year sentence. An additional 7-1/2 year sentence was issued, and to be served concurrently, for Campbell's *habitual* life of crime. Almost twenty years isn't anything to brush off, but in reality, serving good time and behaving himself... Chester did get out much sooner than many of his enemies would have liked. Campbell had learned through books, associates, and of course his own experiences with the prison system, just how the system could be worked for his benefit.

Authorities, however, had secret informants and other witnesses that were gathering information on Campbell's activities since his release in 1983. The question wasn't *if* Chester Campbell was still a bad guy, the question was *how* do you put the guy you *know* is bad away for good when nothing else seemed to work?

The law wasn't the only entity looking to remove Campbell from the streets. In his chosen line of work – there are always enemies. Sometimes those enemies are those thought to be friends. Campbell was smart enough to know the rules of the street. He was a businessman through and through, well aware that danger comes often with a kind word or a handshake. He did not trust his colleagues, but his ego did interfere with common sense. In the past, the police were able to put him away based on evidence that Campbell all but placed on the steps of city hall for them to use against him. He saw himself as above the law, outside the possibility of punishment – even though he had spent the greater

Worked for Italian Mafia Drug Lords

part of his life behind bars. He was dynamic, intelligent, yet very overconfident in his own reputation and skill.

Habitual criminal. That term had been floating around for years – every time Campbell's name was mentioned. It's truly how he Campbell was viewed. Oakland County succeeded in locking him up because he was a habitual criminal, i.e. some of his previous convictions were used against him when sentencing commenced. The federal government was involved now though, so along with the intelligence supplied by informants... they were ready to launch a full-scale takedown of Chester Wheeler Campbell. He was still on parole and the government's informants were taking note of Chester's violations. Based on what these informants were relaying to them - agents from the Drug Enforcement Agency and Federal Bureau of Investigation sought a search warrant for Chester Wheeler Campbell's person and home on Ivanhoe in West Detroit.

The government agreed to protect and utilize three primary informants, with a possible fourth in tow. These informants were known associates of Campbell, all somewhat familiar with his habits and business acumen. Because the FBI and DEA, along with Wayne County officials, had a great desire to remove Campbell from free society, permanently, they took all the proper measures necessary to assure the security and secrecy of their informants and the investigation itself.

If the history behind Chester Wheeler Campbell taught law enforcement anything – it was certainly possible the hit man had paid informants of his own. Campbell was very aware that corrupt entities in city hall, police stations and on the street were extremely valuable in his line of work. Not limited to the knowledge he could gain regarding contract targets, but for his own protection from enemies and the law – intelligence gathering was worth the price. The government wanted to leave no stone unturned, no cutting corners in this investigation. Every possible risk was assessed before they could go after Campbell with ultimate success. Therefore, the maintaining of extremely secured identity for each of the informants was the utmost priority. They were simply identified by code names: FBI 1, FBI 2, and FBI 3. Each of these ultra secretive moles watched, and conspired to observe and relate all of Campbell's activities back to government authorities. One of them directly told agents that Campbell always carried guns, usually a shotgun, in his car. And that's exactly how the law was going to get Chester Wheeler Campbell this time around. He had to be in one of his vehicles.

At approximately 9:00 a.m. on Wednesday July 22nd, 1987 – DEA, Detroit police and FBI agents waited for Chester Wheeler Campbell exit his home on Ivanhoe. Their target emerged from the front door, wearing a black suit and tie. He descended from the porch and walked to the black Dodge Diplomat parked in the driveway, one of two large automobiles he now owned. Chester fired up the car, but did not get any further than just a few feet off his property. As he backed out of his driveway onto Ivanhoe... the government agents descended upon him in a fury. The humid, but otherwise beautiful Wednesday morning became Campbell's darkest day – yet again – thanks to law enforcement.

Guns were drawn and aimed directly at Campbell as he was ordered out of the vehicle. With a disgusted scowl, the suspect exited his car, observing the mass of police in readied positions. Agents quickly secured Campbell, and began the search of his person. Among those present, high profile Detroit lawmen like DEA agent William Coonce and FBI agent Kenneth Walton. The man they came to arrest was, on that day, of very high profile too, and never ceased to amaze and surprise authorities whenever it came to searches.

Neighbors surreptitiously watched as he was being searched. The onlookers could see agents removing items from Campbell's car, but probably had no idea, considering their intentionally distanced perspectives, how vast, unusual and dangerous those items were. Only those persons up close and personal with the search could witness the bizarreness of Chester's possessions.

Chester always had a keen interest in spy equipment and modified weaponry. DEA and FBI were discovering that their informants had only given them the tip of the iceberg on Campbell's collection. Though the information was plenty enough to secure a search warrant in the first place, the agents were amazed at the final tally of weird things Chester Wheeler Campbell kept handy.

First, the basic search of his person uncovered a seemingly harmless, common item. A pen. When the writing utensil was removed from the inside pocket of his suit coat, agents were struck by an unusual appearance. The pen was loaded with a live .22 caliber round. Campbell had modified, or purchased the pen in the revised condition, which enabled it to fire a single round with the push of plunger.

From the back pocket of his slacks, a loaded .32, two shot derringer pistol was removed. Swiftly, agents cuffed Campbell and placed him a police vehicle. Their job was just beginning, as his car and house were going to reveal even more incredible, ominous glimpses into his profession and lifestyle.

Within the Dodge Diplomat, Campbell had six more guns stashed, including a .25 caliber automatic pistol – fitted with a silencer. Searchers found another .22 caliber weapon, a .38 revolver, a .45 caliber, a Colt Python .357 magnum revolver and a pump shotgun. All of them loaded, of course.

But that wasn't all they uncovered in the car. Campbell was hauling two large bags of marijuana, over ten thousand dollars in money orders and loose cash, and heroin packaged in envelopes. The investigators also pulled another large bag from the car, which contained a white powdery substance thought to be at least a pound or more of cocaine or heroin. Campbell's stash was both extremely dangerous and mesmerizing. Agents found explosive devices, gasoline and blasting caps, police scanner, knives (one shaped like the Statue of Liberty), a telescope and video camera complete with all the available trimmings. As if the agents had stepped back in time to the Orchard Lake incident – there it was… a notebook.

Chester never curtailed the incriminating method of record keeping that garnered him so much unwanted notoriety in 1975. Right there in plain view, agents saw a notebook filled with information that included names and addresses of law enforcement, prosecutors, and even a few suspects who were currently being investigated. Campbell still had access to the sort of information that simply makes people nervous.

The search didn't stop there. Into his Ivanhoe dwelling the agents went, and again were in for some stunning finds. From the outside, Chester's home had not changed much since the 1970's. An unpretentious dwelling, with only a few markedly noticeable exceptions – most notably, his house was one of the very few on the street to have a driveway and garage. Property, that's one of the things Campbell kept low profile in his otherwise materialistic lifestyle. He was somewhat of a "flashy" type, and it was obvious Chester loved the finer things in life. When it came to the numerous properties he had interest in, including his home, things were kept more low-key. It was Campbell's collection of dope, weapons, apparel and spy gear that screamed "high end" spender.

When agents entered the home, an elaborate chamber was waiting for their collective "shock and awe" response. One of he most fascinating finds was a room inside that was fashioned like a virtual law office. A desk, typewriter, lamps and a library of books were present in the room. Volume after volume of books was on shelves, each with a universal topic – murder. Investigators estimated Campbell's collection at around two hundred volumes of books related to the subject of homicide alone. Not only did Chester fancy himself quite the armchair attorney... he truly studied like a law student. Criminal law was his primary interest, with an emphasis on the offense of homicide, plus numerous other literary materials relating to crime and punishment, legal procedures and financial topics.

The search continued, turning up the evidence agents had been looking for. Campbell kept inside the house another .357 magnum revolver, a .38 caliber revolver, a .22 caliber target pistol, a .25 caliber automatic pistol with a silencer attached, another silencer (detached), and two 12-gauge shotguns – one sawn off (again very reminiscent of the 1975 findings). Besides the fact some of the guns he kept were illegally modified, a convicted felon is not permitted to possess a firearm – ever. Campbell could've cared less. Furthermore, in his view, the risk of amassing such deadly tools was obligatory to achieve his vocational duties.

Ready for distribution, he had twenty-one bags of marijuana prepared. These weren't dime bags for street urchins to peddle. Each baggy contained one-kilogram of weed; a total twenty-one kilos of marijuana ready for big time delivery purposes. Cops found five thousand in cash as well. The most interesting find however regarded Campbell's advanced interest in espionage. He was always on the cutting edge of surveillance and counter surveillance techniques, and his stash on Ivanhoe showed he had taken to a new mastery – disguise.

Chester Wheeler Campbell's toolkit of cloak and dagger included standard equipment, such as rubber and leather gloves, CB receivers and police scanner. He also possessed a pricey device known as "Bionic Ears" which included a microphone, earpiece for listening and a miniature dish, which was to be pointed in the direction of the subject being observed. The device worked from a distance of several hundred feet, if necessary, to surreptitiously intercept conversations. He also had a tie-clip microphone for capturing in-person conversations to a recording device. Such equipment was expensive and highly useful for Campbell's endless drive to acquire every detail he possibly could.

Remaining incognito was, without question, mandatory for a spying hit man. Since Chester often worked in the same region where he lived and socialized, becoming someone else was very important. To that effect, agents discovered how Chester camouflaged himself: gray false beards, mustache, makeup and a "Design a Face" disguise kit. He basically transformed himself into a harmless looking senior when he wanted to blend in, unnoticed by potential targets or enemies. All of these went hand in hand with his long history of producing various fake forms of identification, which he religiously carried at all times.

The government had their man, and the axiomatic *smoking gun*. None of the agencies involved in Campbell's takedown were going to allow him any wriggle room this time. The last thing anyone wanted was for Chester Wheeler Campbell to wheedle his way to freedom again, ever.

The law had locked him up in Wayne County Jail, but before they could throw away the key, Chester would have, in a sense, one final laugh. The single most inconspicuous item agents pulled from Campbell's car, the one they were sure was smack or blow, well, that one item turned out to be nothing of the sort. The large bag of powder, suspected narcotics they were quite sure, was taken to the crime lab for testing. The results produced no evidence of narcotics of any kind present in the bag. What Chester really had in the container was far more dangerous.

After chemists ran further tests on the powder, it was realized that Campbell was hauling around at least a pound of industrial explosives. Iremite - the trade name of an emulsion form of explosive. This type of powder was ordinarily used for demolition purposes, was definitely industrial grade, and absolutely not available to the general public. Campbell was prepared to do serious damage on someone or something, at some point, if duty called for complete destruction, and surely not for the blowing up of mountainsides.

The infamous hit man was not going to secure freedom this time. The government crossed every *T* and dotted every *I*. This was by no means the last of Chester Wheeler Campbell though. While the law was able to convict him on weapons violations and the habitual prior record was sticking, Campbell was readying himself for the arduous task of composing legal motions. A chore, perhaps, but one he was most accustomed to executing.

CHAPTER TWENTY FOUR

NO REST FOR THE WICKED

"The wicked envy and hate; it is their way of admiring."
- Victor Hugo

CHESTER WHEELER CAMPBELL was charged, convicted, sentenced and shipped off to prison in Wisconsin. His new home? FCI Oxford, medium security prison. For the first several years of his forty-year sentence, Campbell resorted to the old practice of amateur lawyering – handwriting motions, appeals and more lawsuits. He had come to the conclusion that government agencies consistently and intentionally violated his civil rights, wrongfully incarcerated him, and ultimately had absolutely no grounds for his arrest in the first place. Campbell wasn't a young man anymore. A forty year sentence, with no early parole... he would be ninety-six years old by then. It was very unlikely he would ever leave the confines of a prison again, alive that is. He had nothing to lose, and plenty of time to exploit any remote chance of convincing a higher court that he'd been hoodwinked by begrudged officers of the law.

Whether or not Chester ever truly believed the validity his own handwritten legal reasoning would perhaps never be known to anyone except the man himself. He again had a lot of time on his hands though, and his doggedness was quite remarkable, always keeping busy even if it was bizarre legal filings, trying to find some loophole or precedent to offer hope.

Chester's situation looked bleak, but the other prominent Motor City tough guy – Frank Lee Usher – was gaining some legal ground. In another strange twist of events, Usher, while waiting for an appeal hearing in Wayne County Jail in September 1988, was allowed to post bond and literally walked out the door, mistakenly allowed to leave. He was gone for five days, enjoying the taste of freedom. He turned himself in the Marshalls, but his attorney, like everyone else apparently, could not figure out how such a snafu occurred. "By some bizarre set of circumstances," Usher's attorney Steve Fishman said at the time, "they turned him loose."

Just a few months later, Frank Usher was getting legitimate leverage in his fight for freedom. First, Usher's attorney submitted a motion to the court that prosecutors could not use any nicknames during trial, i.e. no mention of "Nitti" or "Big Frank Nitti." Judge Kerwin granted the request. The trial began in the final weeks of March 1989. Kerwin ruled that Usher, having survived the killings, was not sufficient evidence to prove he perpetrated or aided in the murders. The judge did however maintain Usher be tried on lesser charges, which could bring an additional five year sentence.

On March 30th, he was acquitted in the murder, given a thirty to forty month sentence for his plea bargain. Like his one-time colleague Chester Campbell had done so many times before, Usher found himself in a position requiring some serious legal motions. He had been denied time served. The Bureau of Prisons only attributed his prior jail time back to 1988. Usher appealed, but was denied on the basis that he was not in *Federal* custody until 1988, therefore his time served argument was not valid. Basically, even though he was acquitted of the murder charge, the five years he served for the crime did not count because it was State and not Federal prison. Usher saw this, understandably, as a raw deal. Nevertheless, his back was against a wall and would be forced to serve the sentence as the Federal Prison System required.

As for Chester's fate, the media blitz that ensued upon his spectacular arrest in 1987 prompted him to even go after newspaper and television reporters. By 1988, he had filed lawsuits against FBI agents, the media and others on the basis they all violated his civil rights. The courts denied him relief, but Chester appealed. Again, denied. He was most angered by the obvious deceit of his friends or associates that the government was protecting - FBI 1, 2 and 3.

Chester was determined to prove the search warrant used against him in 1987 should be voided. In May of 1989, Campbell's motion to the United States Court of Appeals, Sixth Circuit was argued.

The court wrote of case No. 88-1852: "The question presented in this case is whether deliberate false statements in an affidavit supporting an applications for a search warrant compel the voiding of the warrant even if the false statements are unnecessary to finding a probable cause."

Chester Wheeler Campbell was specifically going after what he thought as 'hearsay' statements made by the FBI's informants. He wanted the court to view the information these informants provided to agents as ineligible for securing a search warrant, thereby negating the whole search.

The court tallied up the list of violations Campbell was guilty of upon execution of the search warrant in July1987. Campbell had been in blatant violation of four statutes, including 21 U.S.C. Sec. 841(a)(1) – for possession with intent to distribute narcotics, 26 U.S.C. Sec. 5861(d) – for having the bomb making materials, 18 U.S.C. Sec. 924(c)(1) – for having a silencer on a gun, 26 U.S.C. Sec. 5861(h) – for his weapons that were stripped of serial numbers, and finally 18 U.S.C. Sec. 922(g) – violated because a convicted felon isn't permitted to have firearms of any kind, at any time at all.

Moving on from there, the court then addressed the issue of Chester's claims. They addressed the District Court's finding that the original affidavit did contain four false statements. The problem however was that the false statements were intentional, to mask the identity of the government informants. Considering the circumstances for which the FBI had to protect the informants, this was viewed as acceptable. Furthermore, informants were not being told information about Chester Campbell by 'other' interposed individuals, but were gathering their information directly from Campbell. The court was comfortable with the elements of this situation. They presented an example of Campbell's points for arguing the opposite by quoting from a line in the request for the search warrant.

"FBI-3 further advised this affiant that FBI-3 learned from an individual who was told by Chester Campbell that Chester Campbell, when in his vehicle, will conceal a firearm in a locations inside the vehicle where it can be easily and quickly reached by Campbell."

While this example was apparently in contradiction to the government's stance, Chester got no relief in District Court because of all the other content in the affidavit was more than sufficient in securing probable cause and search. So, the real issue in front of the court was whether or not there were enough sufficient "untainted" portions of the affidavit to support probable cause. It was called a "Totality of Circumstances" test.

The Court made note of Chester's two primary arguments. Campbell felt, firstly, the original affidavit was null and void because an agent who had graduated from law school, aided by a federal prosecutor, drafted it. He argued that a search warrant should be held to much higher standards.

"The defendant also plays a game of flyspecking that almost no affidavit could withstand," noted The Court in introducing the second of Campbell's arguments. A judge then used Paragraph 4(g) from the original affidavit to illustrate the point:

"During the first week in April, 1987, FBI-3 advised the affiant that FBI-3 has known Chester Campbell for several years and FBI-3 knows through personal knowledge and observation that Chester Campbell carries a firearm when he leaves his residence, especially at night. FBI-3 has observed on several occasions Chester Campbell have in his possession various firearms, described as handguns and shotguns."

The court then presented Campbell's fiery argument for the invalidity of such evidence. Chester's anger had taken his generally professional legal motions to a level of almost manic proportions. Campbell picked the paragraph apart.

"What can the first sentence of the above paragraph possibly mean? Does it mean that every time the defendant leaves his home he carries a firearm? Does it mean that during the several years referred to, the defendant carried a firearm when he left his home? How did FBI-3 know that? Was he present each and every time defendant left his home during these several years? And how long is several years?"

What does the phrase 'especially at night' mean? If defendant carries a firearm every time he leaves his home, this means both day and night. There is no need to state 'especially at night.' And when was the last time that FBI-3 observed the defendant leave his home carrying a firearm. FBI-3 can truthfully claim to have known defendant for 'several years' and still not even seen the defendant for the past 'several years' of the 'several years' that he has known defendant."

The argument morphed into ranting, and the presiding judges were not impressed with the litany of bizarre questions Chester raised. "This is precisely the sort of hair-splitting analysis the Supreme Court has directed the lower courts to eschew in favor of a common sense 'totality of circumstances' test," The Court then stated. "The untainted paragraphs of the affidavit contain information from three independent, reliable informants concerning the defendant's routing possession of firearms on his person."

Chester was not going to get any relief in this case. The Court's decision was that the District Court properly denied Chester's motion to suppress – his conviction was affirmed. As usual though, Chester Wheeler Campbell was not about to give up the art of writing anytime soon. His pen would go into overtime mode in the coming few years, albeit with even more scattered and frenzied memos as the time passed.

Campbell launched more lawsuits, appeals and letters. In 1993, he tried, unsuccessfully, to have a District Court throw out the habitual criminal prior record, dating back to 1976 firearms conviction in Wayne County, based on the fact he was in absentia during the proceedings. A magistrate judge took Campbell's motion as a direct request to 'vacate his sentence' and swiftly dismissed it.

Chester was furious; the prior convictions had continually haunted him for decades and he was throwing everything but the kitchen sink into his legal motions in hopes for some slim chance of leaving prison on his own two feet and not in a casket. However, his efforts were all but entirely exhausted by 1994, so Campbell resorted to writing spiteful tell-off letters. A prominent example of his mindset was in a letter he penned to a circuit judge in the fall of 1994.

Honarable David F. Breck, Circuit Judge
Sixth Judicial Circuit Michigan

People v. Chester Wheeler Campbell, Case
No. 75-22012 (Judge David F. Breck)

Dear Judge Breck:

I call your attention to several other (unimportant) errors of grammar
In your July 11, 1994 Opinion and Order (I am permitted it, you are not).

In the second paragraph of your opinion, page 3, you use "predicate"
Instead (I am sure) of "predicate", on line four.

Also, where you state: the Habitual Fourth charge, when you meant to
Say, either "Habitual Fourth offender charge, or Habitual offender charge."

Since your opinion will not see publication (and thus any comment from

the legal profession, the courts, or the public, I am certain, you could care less; and even less about what I think or say. So be it.

As it is widely believed, in any event, that judges do not ordinary Read their opinions (or even draw them up), I can readily believe that such is

so, in my case. And, particularly, where you did not read the "records and

files" of the case, and base your opinion thereupon, as commanded by the Rule

you cite. Your opinion is an absurdity; and contradictory; to say the least.

So be it.

Sincerely,

Chester Wheeler Campbell, 02658-039
Box 1000
Oxford, Wisconsin 53952

The motions, lawsuits, and letters slowly began to trail off as the years passed. Chester Wheeler Campbell had tried to overturn his convictions, sue all those he perceived as doing him wrong, reclaim his money, and have his habitual criminal status thrown out. The courts were tied up with his requests for years. His writing degraded, going from professionally written and submitted legal motions to angry rants of hypercritical faultfinding. Eventually, he was going to realize his permanent home was a prison cell.

CHAPTER TWENTY FIVE

LEGACY OF A HIT MAN

"The evil that men do lives after them; The good is oft interred with their bones."
- William Shakespeare, Julius Caesar

HE REGARDED HIS own existence as a sorrowful one; at least during the times he was caught in a criminal act. It was his view that fate, society or any number of other factors was responsible for his life of crime. He publicly described himself once as, "one of God's unfortunate creatures." The tragedy of Chester Wheeler Campbell is that he was actually far more a casualty of his own character than any other outside variable. Boosting his overall perception of his own identity and power, the image of charisma and intelligence he most certainly embodied. Smart, sly and methodical. His retribution, for an inarguably difficult early life, was to take whatever he wanted, be it replaceable objects or the irreplaceable human life. Chester was good at it, but arrogance - disguised as confidence - would secure his fate.

When all is said and done – in the life of gangster – there are, with a few rare exceptions, usually only a handful of endings: Death, prison, or turning witness (the latter resulting in a life of forever looking over one's shoulder). Chester Wheeler Campbell never admitted any wrongdoing, but his intricate record keeping, and some past self-serving actions, certainly did implicate others. By and large though, Chester was not a "rat" – the most loathed position in underworld society. But then again, Campbell was the number one target and any other individuals the law wanted, in relation to his dealings, were grabbed up regardless of Campbell's direct help or not. His highly organized methods of record keeping inadvertently implicated anyone and everyone ever associated with him. The Motor City Hit Man had sealed his own fate by being a scrupulous record-keeper. He was also a victim of his own ego. Ultimately, he was not respected or feared by his colleagues enough to override the trepidation law enforcement wielded upon them. Time in prison or cooperate? By the 1980's, many of Chester Wheeler Campbell's associates chose the latter. Times had changed in underworld and how the government dealt with it.

To believe there is unquestioned and unwavering 'honor' in organized crime is perhaps imprudent. One line of advice, as offered by the Georgette Winkler, wife of St. Valentine's Day Massacre perpetrator Gus Winkeler, in her memoirs (*Al Capone and His American Boys*, William J. Helmer) puts this concept in perspective: *"There is no honor among thieves."* Although her writings sat ignored in FBI files for decades until author Helmer put his book together, her suggestion within the tale of what gangster life was really like - that the ideology of 'honor' has always been more myth than truth- is decisive and timeless.

Chester Wheeler Campbell was not the first, and certainly not the last of his kind. Nevertheless, he was perhaps the most notorious, thorough and persistent far beyond the norm within his chosen trade. Chester Wheeler Campbell was dreaded by even those that were accustomed to dishing out a fair amount of fear themselves, and for good reason. He was not without significant successes, such as in the Roy Parsons, Wiley Reed and confiscated money cases (though the latter never produced any relief). Still, in all his efforts to work the system, get one up on the competition, and survive above the law... the Motor City Hit Man was not able to outsmart or intimidate a handful of willing witnesses, his own records and trophies of crime, but most of all – he wasn't able to deny the effects of his own body's betrayal.

Chester Wheeler Campbell had, at some point in his life, contracted the Hepatitis C virus. The hit man had spent a good portion of his adult existence behind bars, but for the life he chose while on the outside also brought him into the sights of the grim reaper more often than not. His profession required direct contact with narcotics, addicts, dealers, paraphernalia, and all the dangerous elements that go along with it, including bodily harm. Chester Campbell had, perhaps, engaged in intravenous drug use himself. He may have contracted the virus from unsafe sexual liaisons (though the medical field considers Hepatitis B more of the 'sexually' transmitted form; Hepatitis C more often from direct blood contact or intravenous drug use). Also a plausible culprit in contracting the virus, especially during the 1970's and early 1980's: receiving blood transfusions. According to statistics on Hepatitis C infections from, www.epidemic.org, "Prior to 1990, there were no tests for hepatitis C against the blood supply, and the rate of post-transfusion hepatitis was between 8% and 10%. Anyone who received a blood transfusion prior to that time is at risk for having been infected."

Although the percentage of infections for intravenous drug

users and "low income" demographics is much higher than that of blood recipients, Campbell had himself been the victim of gun related injuries, multiple times, dating back, at least, to the early 1970's incident when Roy J. Parsons shot him in the leg. His body, from the time of his youth, was beholden to wounds, scarring upon every limb. And then in 1985, obviously the numerous projectiles that penetrated his frame, from head to thighs, certainly caused considerable blood loss. Again, Campbell had undergone eleven hours of surgery following the attempt on his life. He was in a position, on more than a few occasions, to have been the recipient of blood transfusions, thus upping his risk of contracting the virus every time he was seriously wounded.

It is also known that Campbell did partake in alcohol consumption, at least occasionally, and the effects of liquor on the liver – especially a liver already in jeopardy by the virus – would not have helped his health. It took a while, no doubt, for the lifestyle and disease to catch up with him. Improperly treated, or not treated at all, Hepatitis C runs a destructive course on the human body. The slow process of scarring and inflating the liver finally wore Campbell's physical condition down to the point of requiring a special medical facility's care. He was aging, inflicted by disease and certainly on borrowed time. Chester would never see the outside world again.

Many of the landmarks in Chester's old stomping grounds were bulldozed; others left abandoned or changed hands numerous times. Of those figures he was involved with, well, some faded into obscurity – others moved on. Mary Williams, for example, tried a few more times to reinstate the funeral home after several instances of license loss. Her final shot at it ended in 1989 when, again, proper records were not filed and she lost her license to operate. Frank Lee Usher served his time in prison and was released in the 1990's. Last word on Big Frank Nitti... he moved out of state and started over.

Chester Wheeler Campbell was sixty-nine years old: his health deteriorating steadily. The prison in Oxford Wisconsin authorized his transfer to the Federal Medical Center in Rochester Minnesota in March 2000. The center, a minimum-security facility, is known for specializing in management of physically and mentally ill prisoners; this is where the complications of his affliction could be best treated.

The reaper had been patient for a long time. After his transfer to FMC Rochester, Campbell's medical care continued for a little over a year before the angel of death could wait no more. At 6:42 on May 28th, 2001, Chester Wheeler Campbell passed away in the medical facility. His body was promptly sent to medical examiner's office. The coroner, Paul G. Belau M.D., performed an autopsy on June 6th and declared his death 'natural' - by way of *end stage liver disease* – a result of the Hepatitis C virus in his body. His remains were then sent to Macken Colonial Cremation Services, also in Rochester.

Upon his death and cremation, there was no property for anyone to claim. Chester had nothing in terms of assets, nor was he ever married, and no known children. He never served in the military, and though he was known to once have many investments, the only legitimate job he was listed as having – the ironic duty of funeral home driver. He did however leave an incredible tale. A life woven into a corrupt, disparaging and tragic era for an iconic city, his story is both haunting and illuminating. It is fascinating, but disturbing. Most of all, Chester Wheeler Campbell's life story should be an opportunity to truly take a revealing look at how a person can yield into such a dramatically dark and twisted path. Here was a man, a black man, a gangster, an assassin, a master of disguise, a spy, a businessman, a legal assistant, but most of all - an anomaly that essentially struck fear into the very core of Detroit's system law and order. Largely, he was a mythological figure – his story and impact of his existence simply underexposed.

He was dynamic, layered, and a dichotomy – human and inhumane wrapped up in one package. Chester was an investor, a businessman, a legal assistant, a driver. He was also a courier, a dealer, a spy, an enforcer, a ladies man... and a Hit Man.

He was gifted in many ways, although most of that talent used for criminal enterprise. Those skills instilled so much fear and loathing in people from both sides of the law. And yet, how he acquired much of the information is still a mystery; forever Chester's secret. Even on the coroner's cold steel exam table, Chester Campbell left unanswered obscurities. His death notice, for example, referred to his race as "unknown" while identifying him as "Hispanic"– with further notation, "Unknown if Spanish/Hispanic/Latino." Perhaps he will always keep people guessing. In life, Chester Wheeler Campbell liked it that way. He never told the truth if an outcome would be better served by lying; his profession, his associates, his name and physical attributes to name a few such deceptions.

The end of the Motor City's most dangerous enforcer was certainly not the end of the underworld he dwelled in. Drug wars, and the war on drugs, have not slowed since the time of Henry Marzette, Chester Campbell, The Giacalones, or Frank Lee Usher. It can be said that the unlawful domain itself is merely a microcosm, a mirror of mainstream society and economics. What happens in a back alley doesn't differ all that much from what transpires on Main Street, or Wall Street. If that was and is the case, then an explanation exists as to why and how the two worlds intermingle, perhaps to the shock and chagrin of so many. Money – acquiring it, maintaining it, and utilizing it are the common ground element of both illicit and legitimate economics. The undeniable victim is society as a whole. The despair, violence, death, cost, destruction and ignorance… these are the residual effects of the drug problem that is certainly not limited to inner cities, the poor, or any singular ethnic or cultural group. The legacy people like Chester Wheeler Campbell leaves is more profound and all encompassing, with lasting impact on every segment of society, culture, politics and economics.

New and enterprising characters are still out to conquer and become conquered, over and over again. Law enforcement has a seemingly infinite number of battles, at any given moment, in the struggle to control the problem. Still, the dilemma exists. There may never be another Chester Wheeler Campbell per se, but if history keeps repeating itself… there will always be others trying to emulate him or the sinister role he served because drugs like heroin are still in high demand. As long as dope is a viable commodity… the business of dope dealing will continue, as will the need for dangerous enforcers to subjugate obstacles in the path of that business.

Chester Wheeler Campbell
1930 – 2001

ACKNOWLEDGEMENTS

I must thank a few people who, without their help and inspiration, this book would never have been possible.

My wife Jennifer – for always believing in and keeping me on course. You are the best partner and objective advisor one could ask for! For my wonderful daughters Kylie and Natasha, you two inspire me to do my best, more than you probably know. Mom and my sister Ingrid. Vince and Jean Brozack, Debbie and Gary Hunt, Anthony "Harold from Miami" Trout and Alex "The Godson" Farrell (when you're both old enough to read this, I hope you like it).

John Grenke... without your interest and tireless help – I could not have done this. I can't thank you enough for all your advice, research and friendship! A big thanks goes for the amazing support of Patricia Crews and Wilma Simpkins. Judge Alice Gilbert, Scott Burnstein and Michael Bars for the insightful, historical and anecdotal commentary.

To my extended family, friends, colleagues and peers - Seth Ferranti, David Amoruso, Michael "Mick Man" Gourdine, MafiaLife Chris, Mob Candy Magazine, Mark Silverman, Informer

Journal, Knokaround Apparel, Makeda Smith and Chris Jones.

A special 'thank you' to Ron Chepesiuk, Dimas Harya and entire family of authors from Strategic Media Books.

And for every one of you out there – family, friends and supporters - that knew this could be done and backed me up when times were tough – I thank you all from the bottom of my heart.

Most of all – I'd like to thank my Dad. I did it! Hope you can look down and see. Thanks for being the best father a kid could ever have. Dedicated to the memory of William A. Cipollini 1938-1997

PRIMARY SOURCES:

"Non-Certified Death Record." Death Certificate, Rochester, 2001.

"Notice of Levy." Taxes, IRS, 1975.

"Primary Source Evidence Files." Chester Wheeler Campbell Evidence, 1975.

"Sixteenth Census of The United States." Detroit, 1940.

INTERVIEWS:

Bars, Michael, interview by Christian Cipollini. *Attorney* (2013).

Burnstein, Scott M., interview by Christian Cipollini. *Organized Crime Historian.*(2012).

Gilbert, Judge Alice, interview by Christian Cipollini. *Oakland County Circuit Court Judge* (2013).

BOOKS:

Boyd, Robert. *The Streets Don't Love You Back.* Robert Boyd, 2009.

Chepesiuk, Ron. Wilson, Scott. *Straight from the Hood: Amazing but True Gangster Tales.* Strategic Media Books, 2011.

Helmer, William J. *Al Capone and His American Boys: Memoirs of a Mobster's Wife.* Indiana University Press, 2012.

Newark, Tim. *Boardwalk Gangster: The Real Lucky Luciano.* St. Martins Griffin, 2011.

FILM:

DEFORCE: America's Past. America's Future. Detroit's Present. Directed by Daniel Falconer. 2011.

Rollin: the Fall of the Auto Industry and Rise of the Drug Economy in Detroit. Directed by Al Profit. 2010.

PERIODICALS:

Altoona Mirror. "Suspected Drug Kingpin Sentenced." April 30, 1980: 4G.

The Argus-Press. "Court Mixup Freed Killer." February 22, 1989: 3.

Baltimore Afro-American. "Police Say Drug Pushers Ambused Attica Leader." November 16, 1982: 55.

Beaver County Times. "Detroit Chief Claims School Trained Assassins." March 4, 1975: 2.

Capecia, Jerry. "Heroin: The Deadliest Game Has Changed."

New York Magazine, December 4, 1978: 66.

Castine, John. "Slain Woman Had Been Murder Trial Witness." *Detroit Free Press*, December 2, 1986: 3A.

Daily Globe. "Police: Slaying Arranged to Appear Drug-Related." January 24, 1980: 14.

Detroit Free Press. "Charge in Doc Holliday Slaying." April 8, 1983: 8E.

Firestone, Joanna. "Higher Education." *The Dispatch*, March 4, 1975: 5.

Flanigan, Brian. "Ex-Con Carried Tools of a Lethal Trade." *Detroit Free Press*, August 2, 1987: 1.

Flanigan, Brian, McGraw Bill. "KILLER'S ARREST RE-CALLS '75 INCIDENT DUPLICATES EARLIER." *Detroit Free Press*, July 23, 1987: 5A.

Flanigan, Brian, McGraw, Bill. "Confiscated Narcotics Turn Out to be Explosive." *Detroit Free Press*, July 24, 1987: 6A.

Ironwood Daily Globe. "Alleged Hit Man's Trial Starts." June 3, 1975: 10.

Ironwood Daily Globe. "Hit Man Charged With Intent to Kill." March 1, 1975: 10.

Ironwood Daily Globe. "Michigan Tenure Panel Moves on Del Rio Inquiry." June 13, 1975: 1.

Ironwood Daily Globe. "Star Witness Perjures Self." June 12, 1975: 6.

Jet. "Alleged Hit-Man Found Guilty, Could Get Life." July 31, 1975: 25.

Jet. "Detroit Judge Reveals His Life Was Threatened." July 3, 1975: 45.

Jet. "New Detroit Dope Boss Seized by Negro Cops." July 22, 1954: 17.

Jet. "Police 'Illegally' Take $280,000 in Weapons Raid." April 24, 1975.

Johnson, Pamela. "'Happy' Battle Sings for His Life." November 5, 1975: 7.

—. "Detroit's Smack: Police Domain?" *Ann Arbor Sun*, July 30, 1975: 3.

—. "Dope Houses: Cookie Jars for Cops?" *Ann Arbor Sun*, September 3, 1975.

—. "Guilty! 3 Cops, 5 Others in Heroin Conspiracy." *Ann Arbor Sun*, December 31, 1975: 3.

—. "The Dope House At 12000 Livernois." *Ann Arbor Sun*, October 1, 1975: 1.

—. "Why "Happy" Battle is Insecure." *Ann Arbor Sun*, October 15, 1975: 3.

Kinkopf, Eric. "Reputed Hit Man is Hit By Shots." *Detroit Free Press*, May 4, 1985: 3A.

Laitner, Bill; Walker-Tyson, Joyce. "Suspect Charged in Double Killing." *Detroit Free Press*, March 26, 1983: 3A.

Ludington Daily News. "Alleged Drug Boss Guily of Decapitation Slayings." June 25, 1980: 2.

Ludington Daily News. "Detroit School Trained Professional Assasins." March 4, 1975: 1.

Ludington Daily News. "Detroit Underworld Figure Convicted." June 24, 1975: 1.

Ludington Daily News. "Judge Erased Record." October 23, 1979: 2.

Ludington Daily News. "Seven Slain in Detroit 'Drug War'." June 14, 1971: 1.

McClure, Sandy; Walker-Tyson, Joyce; Jackson, Luther. "Doc" Slain While Buying Drinks." *Detroit Free Press*, January 24, 1983: 3A.

McClure, Sandy. "Escapee Held In Slaying of 2 At Wet Side Bar." *Detroit Free Press*, April 7, 1983: 12A.

Michigan Daily. "Seven Killed in Detroit; Drug War Link Possible." June 15, 1971: 5.

The Milwaukee Journal. "Police & Courts." October 15, 1979: 2.

Pacific Stars and Stripes. "Detroit Killer College: Murder in the First Degree." March 6, 1975: 9.

The Palm Beach Coast. "Killer Mistakenly Freed." February 23, 1989: 7A.

Pelt, Derek Van. "Cops and Heroin." *Ann Arbor Sun*, December 3, 1975: 1.

Press Telegram. "Police Hero, Protege Aressted in Roundup of 29 Dope Suspects in Detroit." March 19, 1956.

Record-Eagle. "Ring Supplied Convicts Dope." July 7, 1952: 7.

St. Petersburg Times. "Four Men Sought in Detroit Slayings." June 15, 1971: 11.

Swickard, Joe. "Beheading Defendant On Trial In Another

Case." *Detroit Free Press*, December 1, 1983: 3a.

—."New Trial is Ordered in 1979 Triple Murder." *Detroit Free Press*, September 20, 1985: 11A.

—. "Nickname Tossed Out in Retrial of a Man Called Nitti." *Detroit Free Press*, March 21, 1989: 4A.

—."Retrial Clears Man of Murders: 1979 Triple-Slaying Suspect Now Faces Lesser Charges." *Detroit Free Press*, March 31, 1989: 1A.

—. "Threats to Witnesses Put Justice in Danger." *Detroit Free Press*, December 26, 1983: 3A.

—. "Trial Ordered in Powell Slaying, Snitch Killer Bragged, Witness Says." *Detroit Free Press*, April 6, 1983: 3A.

The Afro American. "Suspect Arrested in Two Beheadings." October 1979: 1.

The Albany Herald. "Detroit Murder School Told." March 4, 1975: 1.

The Argus-Press. "Detroit Makes Heroin Scene in a Big Way." November 1, 1982: 1.

The Argus-Press. "Alleged Drug Dealer in Jam." March 27, 1975: 9.

Argus-Press. "Mistrial in Beheading." April 24, 1980: 9.

The Argus-Press. "Testimony Incriminates Defendant." July 9, 1973.

The Bryan Times. "Female Inmate Drank Had Sex with Officers." October 3, 1981: 16.

The Bulletin. "Seven Young Persons Slain in Suspected Detroit

'Drug War'." June 14, 1971.

The Carolinian. "News Briefs: Death." January 24, 1980: 1.

The Herald-Palladium. "Alleged Hitman Awaits Sentence." June 25, 1975: 24.

The Herald-Palladium. "Kalamazoo Trial Features Shoving Match." June 4, 1975: 8.

The Herald-Palladium. "State Judicial Panel Begins Del Rio Probe." June 12, 1975: 14.

The Holland Evening Sentinel. "Dope Crackdown Nets Two Cops in Detroit Raid." March 19, 1956: 1.

The Holland Evening Sentinel. "Smuggling Case May Be Expanded." July 8, 1953: 1.

The Holland Evening Sentinel. "Trial Ordered for Slaying in Detroit." May 3, 1975: 11.

The Owosso Argus-Press. "3 Ex Detroit Police Cited in Dope Ring." September 5, 1957: 2.

The Windsor Daily Star. "Police Nab Dope Duo." July 10, 1954: 2.

The Windsor Star. "Detroit Club Owner Shot and Decapitated." January 23, 1980: 59.

The Windsor Star. "Police Found Guns, Drugs, Paper Says." February 28, 1975: 61.

The Windsor Star. "Police Told to Return $280,000." March 8, 1975: 46.

Times Daily. "Attica Leader Killed On Outside." December 6, 1982: 2.

Toledo Blade. "Detroit Arrest: Toledo Uniform, Badge Are

Found, Division Reports." March 11, 1975: 9.

Toledo Blade. "Detroit Man Acquitted in Beheading Murders Shot to Death in Bar." January 24, 1983: 8.

Traverse City Record. "Narcotics Crackdown Breaks Detroit Ring." March 19, 1956.

Walker-Tyson, Joyce. "Beheading-Case Figure is Slain." *Detroit Free Press,* January 23, 1983: 3A.

Ward, Francis. "Minorities Rising Fast in Narcotics Heirarchy." April 26, 1973: 19.

—. "Detroit Dope War Casualties Mounting." *Winnipeg Free Press,* June 30, 1971: 50.

Youngstown Vindicator. "Dope Raids Net 30 Tied to Big Ring." March 19, 1956: 8.

COURT CASES:

Chester CAMPBELL, Plaintiff-Appellant, V. Roy C. HAYES; Robert Hayes, U.S. Attorney; Keith Corbett,. 89-1558 (United States Court of Appeals, Sixth Circuit, 1989).

Chester W. CAMPBELL, Plaintiff-Appellee, V. UNITED STATES of America et al., Defendants-Appellants. 75-2372 (United States Court of Appeals, Sixth Circuit, 1976).

Chester Wheeler CAMPBELL, Plaintiff V. Ralph B. GUY, Jr., et al., Defendants. 80-74592. (United States District Court, E. D. Michigan, S. D., 1981).

Chester Wheeler Campbell, Plaintiff-appellant, v. L. Brooks Patterson, et al., Frank J. Kelley, et al., Defendants-appellees. 724 F.2d 41: (United States Court of Appeals, Sixth Circuit, 1983).

Chester Wheeler CAMPBELL, V. Plaintiff-Appellant,Joseph SHEARER, et al., Defendants-Appellees. 82-1665 (United States Court of Appeals, Sixth Circuit, 1983).

Frank Lee Usher, Petitioner-Appellant, v. United States of America, Respondent-Appellee.,. 91-1038 (Sixth Circuit, 1991).

In re FEDERAL GRAND JURY.In re Chester Wheeler CAMPBELL, Petitioner. 92-1430 (United States Court of Appeals, Sixth Circuit, 1992).

People of the State of Michigan V. Chester Wheeler Campbell. CR75-22012 (Ciruit Court County of Oakland, 1975).

The People of the State of Michigan V. Chester Campbell. A81995 (Detroit Recorders Court, 1969).

STATE OF MICHIGAN, DEPARTMENT OF TREASURY, REVENUE DIVISION, PLAINTIFF-APPELLEE,. (Court of Appeals).

United States of America, Plaintiff-Appellee, v. Chester W. Campbell, Defendant-Appellant. 88-1852 (Sixth Circuit, 1989).

United States of America, Plaintiff-Appellee v. Frank Lee Usher, Defendant-Appellant. 82-1113 (United States Court of Appeals, Sixth Circuit, 1983).

WEBSITES:

http://apps.michigan.gov/ICHAT/Printerfriendlyresults.aspx?id+7536270.

http://www.britannica.com/EBchecked/topic/229282/Vito-Genovese

http://law2.umkc.edu/faculty/projects/ftrials/sweet/racesindetroit.html.

http://thecyn.com/heroin-rehab/street-names/. http://thecyn.com/heroin-rehab/street-names/.

http://www.epidemic.org/thefacts/theepidemic/USRiskGroups.

http://www.geocities.ws/jiggs2000_us/morton.html.

http://www.geocities.ws/jiggs2000_us/morton1.html.

http://panachereport.com/channels/black_underworld/index.html.

http://www.pbs.org/wgbh/pages/frontline/shows/heroin/transform.

Scott M. Burnstein, James Buccellato. *http://detroit.cbslocal.com/2011/06/24/organized-crime-in-detroit-forgotten-but-not-gone/.*

http://www2.metrotimes.com/editorial/story.asp?id=2460.

Thomas Hunt. http://mob-who.blogspot.com/2011/04/genovese-vito-1897-1969.html

CURRENT AND FORTHCOMING TITLES FROM
STRATEGIC MEDIA BOOKS

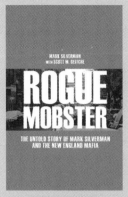

ROGUE MOBSTER
The Untold Story of Mark
Silverman and The New
England Mafia

GORILLA CONVICT
The Prison Writings
of Seth Ferranti

CHILLI PIMPING IN ATLANTIC CITY
The Memoirs of a Small-Time Pimp
and Hustler

SERGEANT SMACK
The Legendary Lives and Times of
Ike Atkinson, Kingpin, and his Band
of Brothers

AVAILABLE FROM STRATEGICMEDIABOOKS.COM, AMAZON, AND MAJOR BOOKSTORES NEAR YOU.

VANISHED:
The Life and Disappearance of Jimmy Hoffa

BLACK CAESAR:
The Rise and Disappearance of Frank Matthews, Kingpin

ESCOBAR VS CALI:
The War of The Cartels